CLEAN SWEETS

With Gluten-Free, Sugar-Free, Vegan, and Paleo Options

Simple, High-Protein
Desserts for One

CLEAN
SWEETS

ARMAN LIEW

The Countryman Press
A division of W. W. Norton & Company
Independent Publishers Since 1923

Manufacturing by Versa Press
Book design by Kisscut Design
Production manager: Devon Zahn

The Countryman Press
www.countrymanpress.com

A division of W. W. Norton & Company, Inc.
500 Fifth Avenue, New York, NY 10110
www.wwnorton.com

978-1-58157-449-4

10 9 8 7 6 5 4 3 2 1

NUTRITIONAL INFORMATION

Please note that I do not possess any official certifications in nutrition, fitness, or the health industry. I have included basic nutritional information for each recipe, which has been cross-checked by two certified dietitians. These measurements are for the ingredients specified in the base recipe (without any of the swaps offered) and will differ depending on what brand or option you choose. Please consult a medical practitioner or registered dietician for personal dietary needs.

CONTENTS

Introduction

I WAS A CHUBBY LITTLE FELLA for most of my life. I grew up in Australia in a family of Persians, Chinese, Malaysians, and Brits, and food was both a reward and a central part of celebrations. By the time I finished college, overweight from years of being sedentary and eating at 3 a.m., I knew I needed to make some drastic dietary changes—changes that would be achievable and that I could maintain.

Exercise came naturally, but sticking to a healthy diet didn't—until I began to realize that through trial and error I was able to lighten up the treats and desserts that were always my diet-downfall. Soon, I was able to enjoy desserts *every single day* as part of my healthy diet.

After extensively developing and experimenting with recipes, I have a firm grasp on what works and what doesn't work in healthy dessert adaptations. Because I blog about a wide range of sweet recipes, I understand what flavors readers appreciate most, and what they find easiest to prepare.

My voice is unique in the large healthy food blogging community. Most male food bloggers do not focus on healthy recipes or ingredients, and my more masculine approach seems to really resonate with readers—both men and women. I also enjoy sharing my family stories, conversations with friends, inspiration for recipes, and day-to-day relatable endeavors in my effort to live a healthy life, and these personal notes have fostered a loyal audience of readers and home bakers.

Cooking and eating have always been a central part of my life, family, culture, and identity. Through *The Big Man's World*, I'm able to share this love and passion in a healthy way.

I am a foodie, and creativity and originality are essential. But most importantly, these healthy substitutions cannot sacrifice taste. Ever.

WHO IS THIS BOOK FOR?

If you are like me and you can't say no to dessert EVERY SINGLE DAY, this cookbook is for you! Every single recipe is healthier than their traditional counterparts, and I've made sure to add a boost of protein in each one, whether that be through eggs, dairy, protein powder, or nuts and spreads. Not only that, I've cut down on as much sugar (natural or processed) as possible, without sacrificing on the taste. Yes, some recipes do call for or recommend real maple syrup, agave, or even coconut sugar, but it's in a much smaller amount. If even that is too much, I've tried to provide a sugar-free alternative if possible. Best of all, every single recipe is 100% gluten-free.

Saying all this, if you are after a dessert-parlor-style sundae, a boxed brownie, or a rich and creamy ice cream, then you'll be disappointed. I want YOU to enjoy dessert multiple times a day, whether that be ice cream as a post-workout snack (the mocha ice cream on page 163), a brownie that you can enjoy for breakfast (I love the breakfast brownie on page 47), or a bakery-style blueberry muffin that you can enjoy between meals (see recipe on page 82). I'm not one to deprive myself, but I'm also wary of what I put into my body, so I'm happy to enjoy a healthier dessert—and even better if it can be for every single meal. As my motto in life states:

Let them eat cake . . . for breakfast.

ABOUT THE BLOG

I started my blog, *The Big Man's World*, as a somewhat random online journal where I shared my meals, restaurants, and other life antics, including thoughts on the human body and the media. Slowly, I started sharing recipes as a means for my own record. I wanted to be able to have all of my random creations stored somewhere for easy reference, and soon enough I had quite the list.

I never, in a million years, would have thought people would actually start making the recipes and start leaving feedback—positive feedback! It was comforting to hear other people who had gone through their own weight loss journey and/or had trouble taming their sweet tooth.

Since July 2013, I've been sharing healthy recipes on my site *thebigmansworld.com*. The longer I blogged, the more I learned what my readers enjoyed: options. While most healthy recipe blogs cater to specific diets—vegan, gluten-free, paleo, sugar-free—I develop one base recipe and then share tested options for *each* of these particular diets, if possible.

G = gluten-free
S = sugar-free
V = vegan
P = paleo

My goal is healthy eating. I personally don't follow a specific regimen but rather experiment with multiple diets. While many of my readers come to my blog in search of dessert recipes with narrowly designed ingredient lists, many of my readers are simply like me: men and women looking to indulge without guilt.

Not using tapioca flour, coconut nectar, xanthum gum, vitamixers, nut grinders, and citrus reamers forced me to step outside the box to create delicious desserts for discerning chefs. This separates me from other bloggers who rely on more expensive and hard-to-find ingredients and gadgets. My recipes can be made the instant the craving starts; no trip to a far-away health food store required.

A Guide to Alternative Ingredients

WHEN CREATING RECIPES for the cookbook (along with most of the recipes on my website), I try to ensure that there isn't a laundry list of ingredients. Furthermore, I try to ensure the key ingredients used have easy substitutions available. These substitutions are based around other similar ingredients, and ones that can be used interchangeably. They don't affect the original ingredient too much, and still result in a very similar final product.

MASHED STARCH BASE

Many of the recipes in this cookbook include a mashed starch of some sort. Below are the ones that can be used interchangeably, and I've also included some handy tricks if you opt to use those instead.

- **Pumpkin:** My favorite base, as it's not overpowering and very slightly sweet. It works fantastically with chocolate recipes.

- **Sweet Potato:** Similar to pumpkin, it's naturally sweeter, and in no-cook recipes it yields the thickest consistency. It's great for puddings, smoothies, and frozen desserts. It also bakes very well.

- **Banana:** Mashed, overripe banana can be used in almost any baked good to add moisture and tenderness. It also works as a great replacement for butter and/or oil. However, unlike the other three bases, it is quite overpowering and unless the recipe is banana specific, you are best to stick to another option.

- **Unsweetened applesauce:** Unsweetened applesauce works well to add moisture to mug cakes and some baked goods. It also works well in less sweet recipes. However, it tends to be less stable and may need a little more dry ingredients (such as flour) to have the same final result as the other starch bases.

NUT BUTTER

Nut and seed butters are the one ingredient that can be used interchangeably in any recipe that calls for a specific type.

- **Almond Butter:** I love using almond butter in recipes that call for chocolate, fruit, or baked goods. It adds a slightly nutty texture and flavor, but does not take over the recipe itself.

- **Cashew Butter:** This is the best nut butter for adding texture to a recipe (from a fat source) without overly affecting the flavor. It's mild tasting, so it mixes very well in most recipes. I recommend a smooth blend.

- **Peanut Butter:** Easily the most accessible and common nut butter, it works for any recipe calling for a nut butter. Like banana, it is overpowering and the flavor is quite evident. I'd use this for peanut butter-specific recipes, or recipes in which you wouldn't mind tasting it.

- **Sunflower Seed Butter/Soy Nut Butter:** Both sunflower and soy nut butter work in any recipe calling for a nut butter, and are a fantastic alternative for those with nut allergies. I'd recommend using a store-bought kind of sunflower seed butter or adding some sweetness to home-made versions, as they can be slightly bitter on their own.

STICKY SWEETENER

Like nut butters and mashed starches, sticky sweeteners have easy swaps that can generally be used interchangeably in most recipes. Some are better for certain types (brown rice syrup for no-bake recipes, or maple syrup for baked goods).

HACK! If you are substituting brown rice syrup in any recipe, you will most likely need to add an extra teaspoon/tablespoon of whichever sticky sweetener you choose, as brown rice syrup is considerably stickier than the others.

- **Maple Syrup:** I refer to maple syrup the most, as it's most accessible and lends a sweet flavor without being too overpowering. It's not overly sticky, so works well in baked goods and cakes. It's best substitution would be agave nectar.

- **Brown Rice Syrup:** Hands down, the stickiest of all the sweeteners, which works fantastic in no-bake recipes. You can also use it in baked goods, but it isn't as sweet as maple syrup, so take note when using it. It also tends to make baked goods a little less fluffy.

- **Agave Nectar:** Agave has a very similar texture profile to maple syrup, however the flavor is less overpowering. It's a good substitution for recipes that don't rely on the sweetness from the sticky sweetener specifically.

- **Honey:** Similar in texture to maple and agave, honey lends a fantastic texture to both baked and no-bake recipes. However, it is very evident and significantly more overpowering than most other sweeteners. Unless you really like an obvious honey flavor, I'd recommend using it as a last resort.

- **Sugar-free Syrup:** Unless you are opposed to using any of the above sweeteners, I'd avoid sugar-free syrup completely (unless the recipe states a tested option). Sugar-free syrups don't have the same capabilities to hold recipes together, and when baked, often lose their sweetness. It's best to use sugar-free syrup as a topping.

GRANULATED SWEETENER OF CHOICE

Unless you are considering aspartame or liquid stevia, you are generally safe to swap out any granulated sweetener of choice in recipes.

- **Coconut Palm Sugar:** My preferred sweetener. It does not taste like coconut, irrespective of its name. It is dark in color and isn't overly sweet.

- **Table Sugar:** If sugar isn't an issue for you, it's the stock-standard choice.

- **Granulated Sucralose:** The best zero-calorie sweetener for any recipe, as it doesn't lose sweetness when baked, and also doesn't leave any bitter aftertastes.

- **Granulated Aspartame:** A less-superior version of sucralose, aspartame does not work well with baked goods—it loses its sweetness at higher temperatures.

- **Liquid Stevia:** I'd recommend using liquid stevia as an addition to a granulated sweetener; I try not to use it in my own recipes, as most brands I've tried turn out to be slightly bitter or overly sweet. Saying that, it generally bakes well, and a little goes a long way.

- **Granulated Stevia:** Similar to liquid stevia, I'm yet to find a granulated stevia that doesn't leave a bitter aftertaste. I know many people find brands that work well for them, so feel free to do so. This bakes well and does not lose its sweetness at high temperature.

- **Monk Fruit Sweetener:** This is my favorite paleo-friendly sweetener. It leaves no bitter aftertaste and works well in both baked and non-baked recipes.

MILK OF CHOICE

You'll notice most recipes call for a "milk of choice." As long as it's not canned coconut milk (or condensed milk!) you can use any milk you have on hand—they will all produce a similar result. Besides cow's milk, here are the other three varieties I recommend and use most often.

- **Unsweetened Almond Milk:** Easy, convenient, and virtually flavorless, it adds a natural creaminess to oatmeal and smoothies.

- **Coconut Milk:** Unsweetened coconut milk is similar to unsweetened almond milk. It doesn't have a distinct coconut flavor, and is relatively low-fat.

- **Soy Milk/Rice Milk/Oat Milk:** I wouldn't recommend these for beverages or frozen recipes, as they tend to be a little thin. They work fine in baked goods and mug cakes.

DAIRY OF CHOICE

Dairy can be a little bit tricky, as different sorts provide different textures. Not only that, but non-dairy alternatives are often thinner and more flavorful, especially in non-baked recipes.

- **Greek Yogurt:** Greek yogurt is the best for any recipe calling for yogurt, and is superior in baked goods and frozen recipes. For baked goods, any fat percentage works (non-fat and full-fat). For frozen recipes, the more fat the yogurt has, the thicker the end result will be.

- **Natural Yogurt:** A thinner version of Greek yogurt, it's best used for baking, as opposed to frozen/cold recipes. It won't give you as thick a result as Greek yogurt.

- **Cottage Cheese:** Unsalted cottage cheese can have a similar texture to Greek yogurt. You will need to blend it before using it, as the curds affect the texture of recipes.

- **Ricotta Cheese:** A mild flavor and texture, it's great for cheesecake-like recipes. Try to use the unsalted varieties—but unlike with cottage cheese, even the salted varieties aren't overpowering.

- **Non-dairy Yogurt:** I'd only recommend this if you cannot tolerate dairy or are following a vegan lifestyle. While it generally works fine in baked recipes, it is very thin in smoothies and frozen desserts.

- **Coconut Yogurt:** Only use coconut yogurt as a last resort or if you follow a paleo lifestyle. It is thin and also has a generally overpowering coconut flavor. It's also relatively expensive.

PROTEIN POWDER

Protein powder can make or break any recipe that calls for it. Every single brand and type on the market differs, so it really takes a significant amount of trial and error to find one that works for you and your recipes. Personally, I've narrowed down three types of protein powders that I've found to work very well in my recipes. You'll notice I've omitted the most common whey protein from the list. Whey protein (from my experience) often leaves baked goods extremely dry, and leaves no-bake recipes extremely sticky. Unless you are having a stock-standard smoothie or using a blend of whey protein (whey mixed with casein and/or other protein powders), I wouldn't suggest it.

- **Casein Protein Powder:** If you can tolerate dairy well and don't have any dietary restrictions, casein protein powder is my first choice. It's thicker than most protein powders on the market, and bakes beautifully. You may need to add more milk/liquid to recipes when using this particular powder.

- **Brown Rice Protein Powder:** This plant-based protein powder is superior to other blends, such as pea and hemp protein. It has a mild taste and, similar to casein, bakes really well. It's also thick when mixed with dairy and in frozen treats.

- **Paleo Protein Powder:** There are several main paleo-specific protein powders on the market. They aren't very sweet, but generally bake well. Paleo protein powder isn't as thick as casein or brown rice protein powder. For no-bake recipes, if the mixture is too thin, add extra coconut/oat flour. For baked goods, be careful with the milk and start small before increasing.

FLOURS

Coconut Flour

Coconut flour is one of my most used ingredients, for a number of reasons. Contrary to what many people may think, coconut flour is not high in fat, as most coconut-based ingredients are. It's packed with fiber and is often considered a lower-carb alternative to standard wheat or white flours. It's also considered to be a good source of iron and manganese.

Per 2 tablespoons of coconut flour:

FAT: 2 grams

PROTEIN: 2 grams

FIBER: 5 grams

Unlike other flours, coconut can be very tricky to work with. In fact, it took me quite a while before I felt comfortable using it. Coconut flour absorbs liquids like a sponge and you need at least 2 to 3 times the amounts of liquids (milk, water, wet starch) to be able to achieve the same texture as non-coconut flour–based recipes. After some practice (and many failed recipe attempts!), I've got a great understanding of liquid ratios to coconut flour and I am able to achieve successful results.

Gluten-Free Oat Flour (see page 23 for homemade)

For all those times you don't want full rolled oats in recipes, oat flour is your answer. Although it doesn't have the same texture and feel of standard flours, it works fantastically in baked goods. Oat flour produces a light and fluffy texture and has a mild taste. It's also not as grainy or as thick. Oat flour is also a fantastic base for no-bake recipes, especially for those skeptical of using any flour without "cooking."

Per 2 tablespoons of oat flour:

FAT: 2 grams

PROTEIN: 4 grams

FIBER: 3 grams

Almond Flour

Almond flour is a grain-free and paleo-friendly flour that consists of ground almonds. It has the same nutritional composition as almonds and adds a fantastic, nutty flavor to recipes. Almond flour is a great source of vitamin E, magnesium, and manganese.

Per 2 tablespoons of almond flour:
FAT: 8 grams
PROTEIN: 3 grams
FIBER: 3 grams

You cannot swap almond flour for coconut flour in any recipe—they need vastly different amounts of liquids. In no-bake recipes, you can swap almond flour for oat flour, but that would alter the flavor profile.

Make Your Own Ingredients

HOMEMADE OAT FLOUR ⒼⓈⓋ

MAKES

4 cups

TIME

2 minutes, or until blended
into a flour

INGREDIENTS

4½ cups gluten-free rolled oats

Depending on your blender or food processor, you may need to stop blending and stir for all oats to be pulsed. Oats can be stored in an airtight container for up to 4 months.

Store-bought oat flour is convenient, but as with all things convenient it comes at a price. Making my own oat flour was a game changer—it not only saved me money but was so easy to do as well! All you need is a blender or food processor and *voilà*—instant oat flour.

Place the oats in a high-speed blender or food processor. Blend until a flour consistency remains.

BASIC PALEO OATMEAL BASE ⊙

MAKES

1 serving

COOKING TIME

Microwave 5 minutes,
Stovetop 10 minutes

INGREDIENTS

1 tablespoon almond meal

1 tablespoon coconut flour

1 tablespoon granulated sweetener
of choice

1 flax egg (see page 26)

½ teaspoon baking powder

1 tablespoon cocoa powder (optional)

¼ cup milk of choice (non-dairy, if
necessary)

*This can be made on the stovetop
too. It can also be bulk made, in
batches of 4 or 8.*

Most of the available paleo oatmeal recipes are based heavily around flax and eggs, which I find to be a little off-putting: why would you want your creamy cereal tasting like EGGS!? I have, however, worked out an easy combination using similar ingredients in many of the recipes above. You can swap this out in place of regular oats (in the oatmeal recipes) to keep it grain-free and paleo!

Prepare your flax egg (see page 26) and set it aside. While the flax egg is gelling, combine all your dry ingredients in a medium microwave-safe bowl and mix well. Add the flax mixture and your milk of choice and mix until the ingredients are completely combined. Microwave for 60 seconds, until the mixture is smooth and creamy. If the mixture is too thick, add a little more milk.

PERFECT FLAX EGG ⊚

MAKES

1 flax egg

INGREDIENTS

3 tablespoons cold water

1 tablespoon whole flax seeds

This may seem more time consuming than packaged flax eggs but it lends a much better texture to your finished product.

Flax eggs are the most versatile egg substitute in recipes. I've found that the way you make a flax egg can really make an impact on the final result. My personal favorite method may be a little more time consuming, but I find it is the most accurate resemblance to an egg in recipes. It also has a milder taste.

Blend your whole flax seeds into a fine powder. In a small bowl, combine the powder with cold water and refrigerate the mixture for at least 30 minutes.

What You'll Need

I MADE IT A PRIORITY for every single recipe to NOT need any fancy kitchen gadgets or uncommon equipment. I also made it a point to provide several tested options.

The main items and tips you will need are as follows:

1. Unless directly specified, you can use either a **blender**, **food processor**, or simply blend in a **mixing bowl** by hand. Ideally I'd recommend a blender. It doesn't need to be a fancy one either. It can simply be one that can blend some frozen matter (frozen fruit, ice cream, etc.) comfortably.

2. **Waffle** and **pancake** recipes can be interchanged. If you don't own a waffle maker, you can follow the same recipe but fry the batter in the pan. You may need to increase your liquid of choice slightly.

3. Any **mug cake** or **microwave**-based baked good can be made in the **oven**. Suggested baking times and directions are listed within the ingredients.

4. Any **microwave**-based warm cereal or pudding can be made on the **stovetop**, unless otherwise specified.

BREAKFAST
REINVENTED

BANANA CHEESECAKE
BREAKFAST PUDDING ⓖⓢ

YIELD

1 serving

COOKING TIME

5 minutes

NUTRITIONAL INFORMATION

Calories 149, Protein 8 grams,
Fat 0 gram, Fiber 3 grams

INGREDIENTS

1 cup low-fat cottage cheese (dairy-free, if necessary)

1 medium banana, frozen

½ cup milk of choice

½ teaspoon vanilla extract

1 to 2 tablespoons granulated sweetener of choice OR liquid sweetener equivalent (1 tablespoon maple syrup OR liquid stevia)

1 tablespoon coconut flour OR gluten-free rolled oats (optional)

For a very thick pudding, add coconut flour or rolled oats to the blender. For an even thicker pudding, refrigerate the mixture for 30 minutes or so.

Ⓥ Use a dairy-free cultured yogurt and add ¼ teaspoon xantham gum.

Pudding is one of my favorite desserts, especially after trying the infamous Magnolia Bakery's version. This version uses cottage cheese for the cheesecake taste and flavor, and for skeptics, you won't be able to tell! I like adding a tablespoon of coconut flour, as I really enjoy a thicker pudding.

In a high-speed blender, combine all the ingredients until a thick pudding texture remains. Transfer the mixture to a bowl and enjoy!

I was always taught never to waste food—and that extended to baked goods! When my breads or muffins were on their last legs, I'd always crumble the (almost hard) pieces into yogurt and let it soften. Now? You don't need day-old muffins to make the parfait. This simple recipe will amp up your boring yogurt and fruit concoctions!

BLUEBERRY MUFFIN
PARFAIT ⓖⓢⓥⓟ

YIELD

1 serving

COOKING TIME

Microwave 10 minutes, Oven 15 to 20 minutes, including assembling time

NUTRITIONAL INFORMATION

Calories 204, Protein 15 grams, Fat 5 grams, Fiber 7 grams

FOR THE BLUEBERRY MUFFIN

1 tablespoon coconut flour

1 tablespoon almond flour

1 tablespoon gluten-free oat flour

2 tablespoons granulated sweetener of choice

¼ teaspoon cinnamon

½ teaspoon baking powder

1 large egg (or 1 egg white or 1 flax egg)

1 tablespoon neutral-flavored oil (or substitute with mashed starch of choice: pumpkin, banana, sweet potato)

1 tablespoon (or more) milk of choice

2 to 3 tablespoons fresh or frozen blueberries

OTHER

½ cup plain Greek yogurt/low-fat cottage cheese/low-fat ricotta cheese/dairy-free yogurt/coconut yogurt

¼ cup fresh or frozen blueberries

This can easily be prepped the night before. The texture will be similar to overnight oatmeal.

MICROWAVE OPTION

In a microwave-safe bowl, combine the flours, sweetener, cinnamon, and baking powder and mix well.

Add the egg, oil (or mashed starch), and milk and mix until fully incorporated. If the batter is too crumbly, add a dash more milk. Gently fold in the blueberries and microwave the mixture for 1 to 2 minutes, or until fully cooked through.

Remove the mixture from the microwave and allow it to cool completely. Once cooled, break the muffin apart into large chunks/crumbles.

Mix half the muffin mixture with ¼ cup of the yogurt and set it aside. In a tall glass or mason jar, start laying your parfait with ¼ cup yogurt followed by the yogurt/muffin mixture. Finish with the remaining half of the muffin crumbles/chunks. Top the parfait with blueberries and a dollop of extra yogurt and enjoy!

OVEN OPTION

Preheat the oven to 350 degrees Fahrenheit.

Follow the directions as above, but bake the muffin in an oven-safe dish or ramekin.

BREAKFAST BLENDER DOUGHNUTS ⒼⓈ

YIELD

1 serving

COOKING TIME

12 to 15 minutes

NUTRITIONAL INFORMATION (WITHOUT OPTIONAL FROSTING)

Calories 314, Protein 29 grams, Fat 8 grams, Fiber 5 grams

FOR THE DOUGHNUTS

½ cup gluten-free rolled oats

1 teaspoon baking powder

½ teaspoon cinnamon

1 tablespoon granulated sweetener of choice

½ scoop protein powder (15 to 17 grams)

1 large egg

2 tablespoons (or more) milk of choice (dairy-free, if necessary)

¼ cup Greek yogurt (dairy-free, if necessary)

FOR THE COCONUT BUTTER GLAZE

2 tablespoons coconut butter, softened

2 tablespoons milk of choice

1 teaspoon granulated sweetener of choice

Feel free to use a muffin tin or small loaf pan. You'll need to adjust the cooking time slightly. Use a toothpick to test when it's done.

Preheat the oven to 350 degrees Fahrenheit, coat a doughnut pan with cooking spray and set it aside.

In a blender, add all the doughnut ingredients and blend until a batter is formed. If the batter is too thick (if you use a casein-style protein powder, this is often the case) add a dash more milk. Allow the batter to sit for 2 to 3 minutes.

Pour the doughnut batter into the doughnut pan, two-thirds of the way full. Place the pan in the preheated oven and bake for 10 to 12 minutes, or until a toothpick comes out clean and the doughnuts spring back slightly.

Remove the doughnuts from the oven and allow them to cool in the pan for 5 minutes, before transferring them to a cooling rack.

While cooling, make your coconut butter glaze by mixing all the ingredients together in a small bowl. Top your cooled doughnuts with the glaze and enjoy!

An entire batch of doughnuts for one person, and they're secretly healthy? You bet! For the same caloric content of a single doughnut from some popular chains, this version provides you more bang for your buck. Fluffy on the inside and tender on the outside, these doughnuts are packed with protein and has a delicious coconut butter–based glaze. No sugary icing here!

Don't have a doughnut pan? These can easily be made in a small loaf pan or muffin tin.

Growing up in a half-Asian household, rice was its own food group. I never would have thought to eat it in sweet form, let alone consider it a breakfast option. However, after overdoing my morning oatmeal, I needed a change. Cooked rice was the perfect substitute and provided a naturally nuttier texture. This can easily be batch cooked and frozen in single-serve portions—it reheats perfectly!

BREAKFAST RICE
PUDDING ⒼⓈⓋ

YIELD

1 serving

COOKING TIME

Microwave 5 minutes,
Stovetop 10 to 12 minutes

NUTRITIONAL INFORMATION

Calories 305, Protein 29 grams,
Fat 4 grams, Fiber 5 grams

INGREDIENTS

¾ cup cooked rice of choice, cooled

½ teaspoon cinnamon

½ teaspoon vanilla extract

¼ teaspoon sea salt

1 to 2 tablespoons granulated
sweetener of choice

1 scoop protein powder
(32 to 34 grams)

¾ cup (or more) milk of choice (dairy-
free, if necessary)

Cinnamon and coconut butter,
to glaze

*Protein powder can be omitted
completely or substituted with peanut
flour or powdered peanut butter. If
you do this, you won't need to add any
extra milk.*

*If you use a sweetened protein powder,
feel free to omit the granulated
sweetener of choice.*

In a large microwave-safe bowl, add the cooked rice of choice with the cinnamon, vanilla extract, sea salt, granulated sweetener, and milk of choice. Microwave for 2 to 3 minutes, watching to ensure it doesn't overflow.

Remove the mixture from the microwave and allow it to cool slightly. Stir in the protein powder and if it's too thick add more milk until you reach your desired texture. Heat for an extra 30 seconds. Top with cinnamon and coconut butter and enjoy!

To make on the stovetop, add the ingredients to a saucepan (except for the protein powder) and bring to a simmer on medium heat. Once warm, gently stir in the protein powder of your choice. If the mixture is too thick, add milk until you reach your desired texture. Continue cooking for a minute before transferring the pudding to a bowl, then top it with cinnamon and coconut butter and enjoy!

This can be made in advance and enjoyed cold, overnight oatmeal style. Simply add extra milk in the morning until your desired consistency is reached.

CHOCOLATE
GREEK YOGURT PANCAKES ⒢

YIELD

1 serving

COOKING TIME

10 to 12 minutes, until all the batter
is used up

**NUTRITIONAL
INFORMATION**

Calories 555, Protein 40 grams,
Fat 14 grams, Fiber 12 grams

FOR THE PANCAKES

½ cup gluten-free oat flour
(can substitute with whole wheat,
all-purpose, or white flour)

1 teaspoon baking soda

¼ teaspoon sea salt

1 tablespoon cocoa powder

1 large egg

¾ cup vanilla Greek yogurt
(dairy-free, if necessary)

¼ teaspoon vanilla extract

**FOR THE GREEK YOGURT
CHOCOLATE SAUCE**

2 tablespoons Greek yogurt

1 tablespoon cocoa powder

1 tablespoon pure maple syrup

Milk of choice, as needed

*If you use all-purpose or self-raising
flour, your pancakes will be much
fluffier.*

*If you use an unsweetened Greek
yogurt in the batter, the pancakes
themselves will not be sweet.*

In a mixing bowl, add the oat flour, baking soda, sea salt, and cocoa powder and mix well.

In a separate bowl, whisk the egg, Greek yogurt, and vanilla extract until well combined. Pour the wet mixture into the dry mixture and stir until fully combined. The batter should be very thick.

Heat a lightly greased frying pan on medium heat. Once the pan is hot, spoon the batter onto it, making pancake shapes. When the edges start to bubble, flip the pancakes and cook until both sides are lightly golden.

Once all the pancakes are cooked, in a bowl, make the chocolate sauce by combining the yogurt, cocoa powder, and pure maple syrup and mixing well until fully combined. If the sauce is too thick, add a dash of milk. Layer the pancakes with the frosting and enjoy!

Ⓢ Use natural/plain yogurt and swap the maple syrup for sugar-free syrup.

Pancakes are one dish people find intimidating and/or time consuming to make. This simple recipe proves otherwise. It uses just a handful of ingredients and has a customizable creamy chocolate sauce. Not a fan of chocolate? Simply omit the cocoa powder and cook as is!

CREAMY TIRAMISU
OVERNIGHT OATMEAL ⓖⓢ

YIELD

1 serving

COOKING TIME

10 minutes (hot version), Overnight
(refrigerator version)

NUTRITIONAL INFORMATION

Calories 357, Protein 37 grams,
Fat 9 grams, Fiber 11 grams

INGREDIENTS

½ cup gluten-free rolled oats

¼ teaspoon of salt

1 cup milk of choice (dairy-free,
if necessary)

½ teaspoon vanilla extract

1 large egg (or substitute with
1 large egg white or 1 flax egg)

1 tablespoon coconut flour
(or substitute with extra rolled oats)

1 to 2 tablespoons granulated
sweetener of choice

1 tablespoon cocoa powder

1 tablespoon instant coffee

1 scoop chocolate protein powder
(optional)

1 tablespoon coconut cream or
softened cream cheese (or substitute
heavy cream or non-dairy cream)

What's better than your morning coffee? Having coffee *in* your breakfast too! This recipe was a happy accident—I'd run out of milk but had a cold latte in my fridge from the day before. I simply swapped out the milk for the latte and was rewarded with a mocha-style breakfast bowl! To take it up a notch, I revamped it by adding a swirl of coconut cream for that added "tiramisu" factor.

FOR THE HOT VERSION:

In a small pan on the stovetop or in a microwave-safe bowl, combine the oats, salt, and milk of your choice and cook until all the liquid is absorbed.

Remove the pan from the heat or from the microwave and let it cool slightly. Add the vanilla extract, egg, the coconut flour, granulated sweetener, cocoa powder, instant coffee powder, and protein powder (optional).

Swirl in the coconut cream, top with extra cocoa powder, and enjoy!

continued

If you omit the protein powder, you won't need as much milk.

For a richer coffee flavor, consider using espresso powder.

℗ Use the paleo oatmeal recipe (page 25) as the base. Add to that the cocoa powder, instant coffee powder, and coconut cream swirl.

FOR THE OVERNIGHT VERSION:

For this version, use the vegan flax seed egg only as this will not be cooked, and I don't want you to eat a raw egg!

Combine all the ingredients in a bowl, limiting the amount of milk to ¾ cup, and refrigerate overnight.

DECONSTRUCTED S'MORES FRENCH TOAST ⒢⒮ⓋⓅ

YIELD

1 serving

COOKING TIME

Microwave 5 minutes, Stovetop 12 minutes

NUTRITIONAL INFORMATION

Calories 290, Protein 14 grams, Fat 8 grams, Fiber 6 grams

INGREDIENTS

2 large egg whites

¼ cup milk of choice (dairy-free, if necessary)

Cinnamon, to taste

1 tablespoon granulated sweetener of choice

2 slices bread of choice

1 to 2 tablespoons (or more) mini marshmallows

1 to 2 tablespoons (or more) mini chocolate chips

Whipped coconut cream/dairy-free yogurt/cottage cheese/yogurt of choice

Crumbled graham crackers (optional)

⒮ Use sugar-free marshmallows and chips. Sugar-free marshmallows do not melt well.

Ⓥ For the French toast mixture, swap out the egg whites for ½ tablespoon of flax meal. Allow the mixture to sit for 30 minutes before adding the bread and following the directions as above. Use vegan-friendly marshmallows (such as Dandie's) and dairy-free mini chips (Enjoy Life).

Confession: I don't enjoy eating French toast straight from the pan. I always find it to be a little too sponge-like, and usually (read: always) will let the toast cool and re-toast it in the morning. However, I've found an even more delicious way to enjoy it: deconstructed style! The key here is topping your French toast with chocolate chips and mini marshmallows while the toast is still warm, so that they ooze between the chopped up toast pieces!

STOVETOP OPTION:

In a small mixing bowl, combine the egg whites, milk, cinnamon, and sweetener of choice. Add the two slices of bread into the mixture and allow them to soak on each side.

Coat a large frying pan lightly with cooking spray and heat on medium. Once the pan is hot, add the two slices of bread and cook for 3 to 4 minutes, flipping halfway.

Once they are cooked, cut the bread into square chunks and place them at the bottom

continued

Ⓟ Use two slices of basic paleo bread but don't toast: simply warm the bread up lightly and top it with dairy-free chocolate chips, coconut cream/coconut yogurt, and chopped nuts.

of a cereal bowl. Top with mini marshmallows, mini chocolate chips, and crumbled graham crackers. Allow the marshmallows and mini chips to melt into the warm bread. Top with whipped coconut cream and/or yogurt of your choice and enjoy!

MICROWAVE OPTION:

Follow the stovetop instructions; however, pre-cut the bread into squares. Pour into a greased mug and microwave for 1 to 2 minutes, or until the egg mixture is fully cooked through.

Top with mini marshmallows and mini chips, until it melts through the bread. Top with graham cracker crumbles, whipped cream/yogurt of your choice, and enjoy!

French toast can be made in advance. They can be frozen in batches and simply thawed before using for the recipe.

I really don't like the word Funfetti—but I do like eating confetti-like foods. This light and fluffy blondie is sneaky. It may look like a classic sweet treat on the outside (and taste like one!) but is packed with nutrients and wholesome ingredients. You can feel good about eating it anytime!

CONFETTI BREAKFAST BLONDIE ⑥Ⓟ

YIELD

1 serving

COOKING TIME

Microwave 5 minutes,
Oven 12 to 15 minutes

NUTRITIONAL INFORMATION

Calories 340, Protein 22 grams,
Fat 24 grams, Fiber 8 grams

INGREDIENTS

2 tablespoons coconut flour

2 tablespoons almond flour

1 teaspoon baking powder

½ scoop vanilla protein powder
(16 to 17 grams)

1 tablespoon neutral-flavored oil
(coconut or canola oil works great)

1 tablespoon pure maple syrup

1 large egg white

1 teaspoon vanilla extract

¼ cup (or more) milk of choice,
(dairy-free, if necessary)

Handful of sprinkles, optional

⑤ Swap out the maple syrup for 1
tablespoon or more of your favorite
granulated sweetener. You'll need
to increase the milk of choice by a
tablespoon or two.

MICROWAVE OPTION:

Grease a microwave-safe bowl and set it aside.

In a small mixing bowl, combine the dry ingredients and mix well. Add the oil and maple syrup, mix, and set aside.

In a separate small bowl, add the egg white, vanilla extract, and ¼ cup of milk and whisk lightly. Pour this into the dry mixture and mix well until fully incorporated. If the mixture is too thick, slowly add more milk, one tablespoon at a time, until a batter is formed.

Stir in the sprinkles and pour mixture into microwave-safe bowl. Microwave for 1 to 2 minutes, or until the blondie is fully cooked through.

OVEN OPTION:

Preheat the oven to 350 degrees Fahrenheit.

Follow the microwave directions, but place the batter in an oven-safe dish (the deeper the better) and bake for 12 to 15 minutes, or until a toothpick comes out clean.

I recommend using a large ceramic bowl, as it prevents overflow and can easily be dressed up with berries, yogurt, etc.

If your protein powder is unsweetened, you may want to add an extra tablespoon or two of granulated sweetener of choice.

Almond flour can be subbed with gluten-free oat flour, but it comes out a little more flat.

GRANOLA CLUSTERS ⑥Ⓥ

YIELD

1 serving

COOKING TIME

12 to 15 minutes, or until golden brown

NUTRITIONAL INFORMATION

Calories 332, Protein 16 grams, Fat 14 grams, Fiber 7 grams

INGREDIENTS

½ cup gluten-free rolled oats

1 teaspoon chia seeds

¼ scoop protein powder

1 tablespoon peanut butter

1½ teaspoons pure maple syrup

2 tablespoons milk of choice

I tried making this in the microwave but found it to be too soggy. If you intend to mix it with milk, this would work well.

⑤ Using a sugar-free syrup doesn't work well, as it doesn't have the natural thickness. Omit it completely and slightly increase the milk of your choice until a thick mixture is formed. Post cooking, stir in a tablespoon of granulated sweetener of your choice.

Preheat the oven to 350 degrees Fahrenheit and line a cookie sheet or baking tray with parchment paper and set it aside.

In a small mixing bowl, add the gluten-free rolled oats, chia seeds, and protein powder and mix well.

In a microwave-safe bowl or on the stovetop, mix your peanut butter and maple syrup and heat until they are melted. Whisk in your milk of choice.

Pour the wet mixture into the dry oat mixture until the oats fully coated and sticky. Transfer the mixture to the lined baking tray and spread it out in a single layer. For thicker clusters, do not separate the mixture too much. Bake for 10 to 12 minutes, until it turns golden brown. Allow it to cool slightly before breaking it into clusters.

Among many of my foodie friends, granola gets the crown for being the cereal many of us can't stop eating at one serving. How do we combat that? Make it single serving! This recipe also takes into account the best parts of granola: the clusters.

Growing up, chili sauce and red pepper flakes were a condiment on the same level of salt and pepper. However, enjoying it in a sweet recipe was preposterous . . . until now! For flavor lovers, this one is for you. The slight addition of cayenne will have your taste buds dancing, not to mention the fact that it's a mousse designed for breakfast. Can't handle the heat? Simply leave it out.

MEXICAN HOT CHOCOLATE BREAKFAST MOUSSE ⒼⓋⓅ

YIELD

1 serving

COOKING TIME

10 minutes, including minimum time
to thicken

NUTRITIONAL INFORMATION

Calories 328, Protein 30 grams,
Fat 2 grams, Fiber 12 grams

INGREDIENTS

1 cup mashed sweet potato
(can substitute with pumpkin)

2 tablespoons cocoa powder

1 tablespoon maple syrup

1 scoop protein powder (32 to 34
grams)

¼ teaspoon cayenne pepper

Milk of choice, as needed

Nuts/nut butter/toppings of choice

*For a sweeter mousse, feel free to
increase the maple syrup by an extra
tablespoon or two. If you do, you'll
need less or even no milk to thin out
the mousse.*

Ⓢ Use sugar-free maple syrup
or 1 tablespoon of your favorite
granulated sweetener.

Add all the ingredients into a high-speed
blender and blend until your desired consistency is reached (for a thicker mousse, start
with just 1 tablespoon of milk). Continue to
add milk until desired texture is achieved.

Pour the mousse into a bowl and allow it
to sit for 5 minutes to thicken.

*If you don't have access to a blender, this can easily
be made in a mixing bowl too.*

*This can also be prepped in advance and
refrigerated—the mousse will thicken beautifully.*

RAW COOKIE DOUGH
BREAKFAST BITES ⒼⓈⓋⓅ

YIELD

1 serving

COOKING TIME

5 minutes, plus additional time to firm up

NUTRITIONAL INFORMATION

Calories 491, Protein 38 grams, Fat 21 grams, Fiber 7 grams

INGREDIENTS

¼ cup gluten-free oat flour

1 scoop protein powder (32 to 34 grams)

1 tablespoon granulated sweetener of choice

2 tablespoons smooth nut butter of choice

1 to 2 tablespoons "add-ins" of choice (chocolate chips/trail mix/nuts, etc.)

¼ cup (or more) milk of choice (dairy-free, if necessary)

This can easily be prepped in advance or made in a bigger batch for quick grab-and-go snacks.

You can swap out the granulated sweetener for a liquid sweetener such as maple syrup. If you do this, you should be able to reduce your milk of choice.

Ⓟ *Swap out the oat flour for almond flour OR 2 tablespoons of coconut flour.*

These raw cookie dough bites were one of my go-to recipes when I worked in an office environment—I used to prep a batch the night before, chuck them in the freezer, and remove them before heading to work. By the time I arrived, I had delicious, thawed cookie dough bites for breakfast!

In a mixing bowl, add the dry ingredients and mix until combined.

Stir in your nut butter of choice until a crumbly texture remains. Add your add-ins of choice and, a tablespoon at a time, add your milk of choice until a thick, firm batter is formed.

Using your hands, form small bites and either enjoy immediately or refrigerate to firm up.

Paying $10 for an off-brand waffle maker was one of my best investments. In my early days of healthy eating, I loved making pancakes but lacked the skills to flip them nicely. Enter the waffle maker, which left me with even better results with much less work!

SEA SALT DARK CHOCOLATE WAFFLES ⑥ⓟ

YIELD

1 serving

COOKING TIME

12 to 15 minutes, depending on waffle maker

NUTRITIONAL INFORMATION (WAFFLE BASE)

Calories 221, Protein 27 grams, Fat 5 grams, Fiber 11 grams

FOR THE WAFFLE BASE

3 tablespoons coconut flour, sifted

2 tablespoons dark cocoa powder

½ scoop protein powder (16 to 17 grams)

1 to 2 tablespoons granulated sweetener of choice

½ teaspoon baking powder

3 egg whites OR 2 large eggs

2 tablespoons (or more) milk of choice (dairy-free, if necessary)

FOR THE SALTED CARAMEL SAUCE

½ cup coconut palm sugar

2 tablespoons water

1 tablespoon coconut oil

Sea salt, to taste

FOR THE DARK COCOA SAUCE

1 tablespoon dark cocoa powder

1 tablespoon granulated sweetener of choice

1 to 2 tablespoons (or more) milk of choice (dairy-free, if necessary)

In a large mixing bowl, combine the coconut flour, cocoa powder, protein powder, and granulated sweetener of choice and mix well. Add the eggs and, using a tablespoon at a time, slowly add in the milk of choice until a thick batter is formed.

Turn on the waffle iron and once hot, pour in the batter and cook through.

Once cooked through, transfer the waffle to a plate and top with the salted caramel sauce and dark cocoa sauce.

To make the salted caramel sauce, heat a saucepan with the water and sugar until it begins to boil, making sure to stir constantly. Add the sea salt and coconut oil and continue stirring, on medium heat, until it thickens. Once it has thickened, remove from the heat.

For the dark cocoa sauce, add your cocoa powder and granulated sweetener of choice in a small mixing bowl. Slowly add milk of choice until it reaches a thick and drippy consistency.

The salted caramel sauce makes much more than necessary for the recipe. Store leftovers in the refrigerator. Alternatively, use your favorite store-bought or sugar-free caramel syrup.

Waffles can be batch cooked and frozen for quick grab-and-go breakfasts/snacks—they freeze and thaw beautifully.

Ⓢ Use sugar-free caramel syrup/sauce.

Ⓥ Swap out the egg whites for 1 flax egg, and increase the vegan milk of choice until a thick batter is formed.

THICK AND FLUFFY VEGAN PANCAKES ⒼⓈⓋ

YIELD
1 serving

COOKING TIME
15 minutes

NUTRITIONAL INFORMATION
Calories 238, Protein 12 grams,
Fat 3 grams, Fiber 6 grams

INGREDIENTS
½ cup gluten-free all-purpose flour
(or substitute with oat flour)

2 tablespoons vanilla protein powder

1½ teaspoons baking powder

1 tablespoon granulated sweetener
of choice (or substitute with a liquid
sweetener of choice)

¼ teaspoon sea salt

¼ cup (or more) non-dairy milk of
choice (if not vegan, can use any
milk)

*If you use all-purpose or self-raising
flour, the pancakes will be much
fluffier. Adjust the milk accordingly.
You want to start off with a too-thick
batter than too runny. If your batter
is too runny, add a little bit more
flour.*

I was always taught that the key to fluffy pancakes was nothing more than the humble egg. However, through experimentation and playing with various flour/liquid ratios, I was able to come up with a stack of egg-free pancakes that could easily stand in for their egg-filled counterparts.

In a mixing bowl, add the flour, protein powder, baking powder, and granulated sweetener of choice and mix well.

Add milk to the dry mixture. If the batter is too thick, add a little more milk until a thick yet pourable mixture remains.

Heat a lightly greased frying pan on medium heat. Once the pan is hot, pour batter and cook until bubbles start to appear on the edges. Flip and continue cooking until both sides are lightly golden.

CREAMY CAKES AND CRUMBLES

BANANA LEMON CHEESECAKE ⓖⓢ

YIELD

1 serving

COOKING TIME

5 minutes, plus 30 minutes to firm up

NUTRITIONAL INFORMATION

Calories 149, Protein 8 grams,
Fat 0 grams, Fiber 3 grams

INGREDIENTS

1 large frozen banana, chopped

1 teaspoon lemon juice

1 teaspoon cinnamon

2 tablespoons milk of choice
(dairy-free, if necessary)

¼ cup smooth fat-free ricotta cheese
OR cottage cheese

1 tablespoon sweetener of choice
(optional)

*You can substitute the ricotta
cheese with Greek yogurt, but
the consistency will be smoother.
Consider blending the mixture until
the yogurt is slightly immersed.*

*For a sweeter cheesecake, increase
the sweetener. I actually omit it, as I
find the banana sweet enough.*

Ⓥ Ⓟ Swap out the ricotta cheese for
cultured coconut yogurt. You may
want to add a pinch of arrowroot
starch to thicken, as the yogurt is not
thick to begin with.

This recipe started out as a cheesecake ice cream experiment, but after several trials I found it to be much better suited as just a cheesecake. The texture, once chilled, was firm, creamy, and perfect as a pre-bed snack—thanks to the dairy!

In a high-speed blender or food processor, add all the ingredients and blend until a thick consistency remains.

Transfer the mixture to a bowl or glass and refrigerate it for 30 minutes to firm up.

FROSTED CINNAMON ROLL BAKE ⓖⓥ

YIELD

1 serving

COOKING TIME

Microwave 5 minutes,
Oven 12 to 15 minutes

**NUTRITIONAL INFORMATION
(USING THE SECOND PROTEIN
FROSTING)**

Calories 253, Protein 19 grams,
Fat 7 grams, Fiber 6 grams

INGREDIENTS

¼ cup gluten-free oat flour

½ teaspoon baking powder

¼ teaspoon cinnamon

1 tablespoon pure maple syrup

1½ teaspoons nut butter of choice

3 tablespoons unsweetened
applesauce

**HIGH PROTEIN FROSTING
(OPTION ONE)**

½ cup Greek yogurt OR smooth
cottage cheese OR smooth ricotta
cheese (dairy-free, if necessary)

1 tablespoon granulated sweetener
of choice

¼ teaspoon cinnamon

**HIGH PROTEIN FROSTING
(OPTION TWO)**

½ scoop vanilla protein powder of
choice (16 to 17 grams)

¼ teaspoon cinnamon

1 tablespoon (or more) milk of choice
(dairy-free, if necessary)

Lightly grease a microwave-safe bowl and add the dry ingredients. Mix well and set the bowl aside.

In a separate small bowl, combine the maple syrup, nut butter, and unsweetened applesauce and mix well. Combine this wet mixture with your dry mixture and mix until fully combined. If the batter is too thick, add an extra tablespoon of unsweetened applesauce.

Microwave the batter for 1 to 2 minutes, or until it's just cooked in the center. Remove the batter from the microwave and allow it to cool slightly.

While the cinnamon bake is cooling, prepare the protein frosting mixture. Combine all the ingredients in a small bowl and mix until a thick frosting remains. Top the cinnamon bake with the frosting and enjoy!

You can substitute the applesauce with mashed banana or a milk of your choice, but adjust accordingly. If you opt for the second protein frosting option, you may need more milk, depending on the brand of protein powder you use.

A quick and easy snack or after-dinner treat, this frosted cinnamon roll bake tastes like the classic! The base can be mixed by hand or in a blender and has easy substitutions. For the frosting, you can either use protein powder or slightly sweeten a dairy of your choice—I personally love using Greek yogurt.

Breakfast, dessert, wholesome snack—this mixed berry crisp fits the bill! Unlike traditional crisps, it doesn't contain any butter or oil, but still has the rich flavor. It's also grain-free, thanks to the combination of almond and coconut flours. If you'd like to batch-cook it, you can easily do so by doubling, tripling, or quadrupling the ingredients.

MIXED BERRY CRISP ⒼⓋⓅ

YIELD

1 serving

COOKING TIME

12 to 15 minutes

NUTRITIONAL INFORMATION

Calories 293, Protein 14 grams,
Fat 15 grams, Fiber 9 grams

INGREDIENTS

1 cup fresh berries of choice*

1 teaspoon lemon juice

2 tablespoons almond flour

1 tablespoon coconut flour

1 tablespoon granulated sweetener of choice

1 tablespoon protein powder (optional)

Cinnamon, to taste

1 tablespoon cashew butter, melted

1½ teaspoons pure maple syrup

You can use frozen berries, just be sure to thaw one cup.

This can be enjoyed cooled, from the refrigerator.

Ⓢ Swap the maple syrup for an extra tablespoon of nut butter or milk of choice, if preferred. This is being used only as a binder, not for taste or texture.

Preheat the oven to 350 degrees Fahrenheit. Grease a small baking dish with cooking spray and set it aside.

In a small mixing bowl, coat the mixed berries with the lemon juice, mix well, then transfer to the greased baking dish and spread out evenly.

In a separate bowl, combine the dry ingredients and mix well. Stir in the melted cashew butter and maple syrup until a crumbly texture remains.

Cover the mixed berries with the "crumble" mixture and bake for 12 to 15 minutes, or until the crumbles are golden brown.

Allow the crisp to cool for 5 minutes and serve with Greek yogurt or ice cream!

RASPBERRY MOUSSE WITH COCONUT FLOUR CRUST ⒼⓋⓅ

YIELD
1 serving

COOKING TIME
15 minutes

NUTRITIONAL INFORMATION
Calories 269, Protein 19 grams,
Fat 13 grams, Fiber 8 grams

INGREDIENTS

For the crust:

1 tablespoon coconut flour

1 tablespoon almond flour

1 tablespoon nut butter of choice

1 tablespoon pure maple syrup

Milk, as needed (dairy-free, if
necessary)

For the raspberry mousse:

½ cup plain Greek yogurt

½ cup fat-free cottage cheese
(dairy-free, if necessary)

¼ teaspoon vanilla extract

1 to 2 tablespoons granulated
sweetener of choice

2 tablespoons raspberries, divided

1 tablespoon coconut flour

*The raspberry mousse thickens when
left to sit. If you want to enjoy it later,
keep the mousse separate from the
crust until you're ready to eat to
prevent it from becoming soggy.*

Ⓖ Omit the maple syrup and
increase your milk of choice.

Piecrusts and dessert crusts
are usually based on flour, butter,
and a boat-load of sugar. However,
shouldn't they just be a vehicle for
the pudding on top? This version
is delicious enough to eat on its
own. We don't do things in halves
here though: a creamy raspberry
mousse on top makes this the
perfect portioned dessert (or even
breakfast)! If you are making it for
more than one, it can also easily be
adjusted.

In a small bowl, add all the crust ingredients except for the milk. Mix until a crumbly texture remains. Slowly add your milk of choice until a thick batter is formed. Transfer the batter to a cereal bowl or tall glass and set it aside.

In a blender, add all the mousse ingredients and blend until fully immersed and smooth. Pour the blended mixture into the cereal bowl or glass, top with the rest of the raspberries, and enjoy!

PEANUT BUTTER CHEESECAKE MOUSSE ⓖⓥ

YIELD

1 serving

COOKING TIME

5 minutes

NUTRITIONAL INFORMATION

Calories 259, Protein 19 grams,
Fat 16 grams, Fiber 2 grams

INGREDIENTS

½ cup plain non-fat yogurt
(dairy-free, if necessary)

2 tablespoons peanut butter

1 tablespoon honey or maple syrup
or granulated sweetener of choice

*For a lower fat option, swap out the
peanut butter for peanut flour. It will
be much thicker.*

*For a thicker mousse, refrigerate
overnight.*

Ⓢ You can use a sugar-free syrup,
but it will no longer be thick. I'd
recommend opting for a tablespoon
of your favorite granulated sweetener
of choice.

Ⓟ Use cultured coconut yogurt, swap
the peanut butter for drippy almond
butter, and enjoy!

The perfect snack that only
takes minutes to whip up: it's
smooth, creamy, and can be even
more protein packed! For an even
bigger hit of protein, feel free to add
some peanut flour or some protein
powder. For a thicker consistency,
let the mousse sit in the fridge for
several hours.

In a mixing bowl, combine all the ingredients
and mix until fully combined.

Transfer the mixture to a serving bowl, top
with extra peanuts/peanut butter, and enjoy!

STRAWBERRY CHEESECAKE MOUSSE ⑤⑤

YIELD

1 serving

COOKING TIME

5 minutes

NUTRITIONAL INFORMATION

Calories 192, Protein 27 grams,
Fat 2 grams, Fiber 2 grams

INGREDIENTS

1 cup low-fat or fat-free cottage cheese

½ cup fresh strawberries

1 tablespoon maple syrup or granulated sweetener of choice

2 tablespoons milk of choice (dairy-free, if necessary)

I prefer using a simple handheld mixer, as it produces an extremely fluffy, mousse-like texture.

For a thicker mousse, blend until just immersed. For a creamier, more pudding-like mousse, continue blending until extremely smooth.

You can swap out the cottage cheese for a Greek yogurt. If you do this, omit the milk of choice, unless you want an almost smoothie-like texture.

Ⓥ Substitute the cottage cheese with cultured dairy-free yogurt.

Ⓟ Substitute the cottage cheese with cultured coconut yogurt and increase the sweetener by 1 tablespoon.

Cottage cheese gets a bad rap for being bland and boring, strictly a diet food. However, when you mix it with a few easy ingredients, it lends a delicious tartness—like in this cheesecake mousse! I personally love making this the night before, as refrigerating it overnight allows it to firm up nicely.

Using a handheld mixer or blender, immerse all the ingredients until thick and fluffy.

Transfer the mixture to a bowl and enjoy immediately.

PEACHES AND CREAM BREAD PUDDING ⊙

YIELD

1 serving

COOKING TIME

Microwave 5 minutes,
Oven 12 to 15 minutes

NUTRITIONAL INFORMATION

Calories 149, Protein 13 grams,
Fat 2 grams, Fiber 3 grams

INGREDIENTS

1 large egg white

¼ cup plus 2 tablespoons milk of choice

1 tablespoon maple syrup

1 slice bread of choice, chopped into squares

¼ cup diced peaches (approximately 1 large peach)

¼ cup plain yogurt of choice

Cinnamon, to taste

1 tablespoon granulated sweetener of choice

If you prefer a moist bread pudding, increase the milk of your choice to ¼ cup, post cooking.

For a sweeter bread pudding, add an extra tablespoon of maple syrup or of a granulated sweetener of your choice.

The next time you buy a loaf of bread, leave a slice or two out to dry up. Why? To make bread pudding! The dry bread soaks up the creamy liquid and is a texture lover's dream. This healthy take on the classic is perfectly suitable for breakfast, especially topped with some protein-packed yogurt or coconut cream.

OVEN OPTION:

Preheat the oven to 350 degrees Fahrenheit.

Grease a large, oven-safe ramekin with cooking spray.

In a small mixing bowl, mix the egg white, ¼ cup of your milk of choice, and the maple syrup until combined. Add the chopped bread and mix until it's fully coated.

Remove the bread from the wet mixture and place at the bottom of the greased ramekin. Pour the excess milk mixture over the bread. Top the dish with the diced peaches and bake for 10 to 15 minutes, until the bread has turned golden brown.

While the bread pudding is baking, whisk

continued

Ⓢ Swap the maple syrup for 1 tablespoon of granulated sweetener of your choice.

Ⓥ Omit the egg whites and add a teaspoon of flax to the milk. Allow the milk to set very slightly before following the directions above. I found it got dry a little too quickly, so consider adding extra milk post baking.

Ⓟ Use 1 slice of paleo bread (recipe at the back). Omit the egg white from the mixture and decrease the milk by 2 tablespoons (the bread is quite moist to begin with). Post baking, add your desired amount of milk.

the plain yogurt with the sweetener and cinnamon in a small bowl.

Remove the ramekin from the oven and immediately top with the extra 2 tablespoons of milk. Top with the "cream" and enjoy immediately!

MICROWAVE OPTION:

Follow the instructions above and microwave for 2 minutes. Remove the dish from the microwave and add 2 tablespoons of milk. You will likely need to increase the milk by a tablespoon or two, if it comes out a little drier.

For all of you fearful of a baking fail, this recipe has your name on it. Typically, strawberry shortcakes are the most beautiful desserts. However, when we're making our own, we don't care TOO much about aesthetics! This one involves crumbling up cake pieces and laying it with strawberries and a dairy base of choice.

STRAWBERRY SHORTCAKE ⓖⓥⓟ

YIELD

1 serving

COOKING TIME

Microwave 5 minutes, Oven 12 to 15 minutes, plus time to assemble

NUTRITIONAL INFORMATION

Calories 218, Protein 11 grams, Fat 15 grams, Fiber 4 grams

FOR THE CAKE

1 tablespoon coconut flour

¼ teaspoon baking powder

¼ teaspoon sea salt

1 tablespoon coconut oil
(or substitute with any neutral-flavored oil, such as canola)

1 tablespoon maple syrup

¼ teaspoon vanilla extract

1 large egg white

1 tablespoon (or more) milk of choice
(dairy-free, if necessary)

FOR THE LAYERS

¼ cup strawberries

¼ cup yogurt of choice (I used a vanilla Greek yogurt)

Using a deep cereal bowl to make the cake work best.

I preferred to let the cake cool completely and crumble it up before building the layers.

If you use an unsweetened yogurt, consider stirring in some sweetener of your choice.

Grease a small microwave-safe bowl and set it aside.

In a small mixing bowl, add the dry ingredients and mix well. Add the wet ingredients and, if the batter is too crumbly, increase the milk of your choice.

Microwave the batter for 1 to 2 minutes, until it's fully cooked.

Remove the cake from the microwave and allow it to cool. Once it's cool, cut the cake in half, layer it with strawberries and the yogurt of your choice, and enjoy!

Ⓢ Swap for sugar-free syrup or 1 tablespoon of granulated sweetener of your choice.

Ⓥ Omit the egg white and increase the milk of your choice until a thick batter is formed. It will be slightly flat.

I can't believe that I used to despise cherries for most of my childhood. I think it stemmed from a cherry-flavored children's cough syrup, of which cherry-flavored candy reminded me. Now? It's my favorite addition to crumbles, as the tartness pairs well with the crunchy crumble topping. This lighter version uses no butter, and just a teaspoon of maple syrup for some natural sweetness.

TART CHERRY CRUMBLE ⓖⓥⓟ

YIELD

1 serving

COOKING TIME

Microwave 5 minutes,
Oven 10 to 12 minutes

NUTRITIONAL INFORMATION

Calories 183, Protein 9 grams,
Fat 6 grams, Fiber 5 grams

INGREDIENTS

¾ cup fresh or frozen pitted cherries

1 teaspoon lemon juice

¼ teaspoon sea salt

1½ teaspoons coconut flour

1 tablespoon gluten-free quick oats

1 tablespoon protein powder
(optional)

½ teaspoon cinnamon

1 teaspoon pure maple syrup

1 teaspoon oil of choice (coconut or
canola works great)

*This can be made in the microwave,
although the crumble topping won't
be as crisp as the oven.*

Ⓢ Use a sugar-free syrup or a dash of
liquid to achieve a crumble texture.
Alternatively, increase the oil by an
extra teaspoon. This will ensure that
the crumble comes out crisper.

Ⓟ Swap the quick oats for almond
flour.

Preheat the oven to 350 degrees Fahrenheit.

Grease a small, oven-safe dish and add the cherries, lemon juice, and sea salt and mix well.

In a small bowl, mix the coconut flour, quick oats, protein powder, and cinnamon. Add the maple syrup and oil and mix until a crumble remains. Pour the crumble on top of the cherry mixture and bake in the preheated oven for 10 to 12 minutes until the crumble is golden brown on top.

WHIPPED TIRAMISU ⒼⓈⓋⓅ

YIELD

1 serving

COOKING TIME

5 minutes

NUTRITIONAL INFORMATION

Calories 151, Protein 19 grams,
Fat 6 grams, Fiber 5 grams

INGREDIENTS

3 ounces silken tofu

2 tablespoons cocoa powder

½ scoop chocolate protein powder
(16 to 17 grams)

1 teaspoon instant coffee or espresso
powder

1 tablespoon coconut cream or
cream cheese (or substitute with
thickened cream or soy cream)

1 tablespoon granulated sweetener
of choice

¼ teaspoon sea salt

1 to 2 tablespoons milk of choice
(dairy-free, if necessary)

*You can easily prepare this in
advance and allow it to chill (this will
also thicken it considerably).*

*You can omit the cream or coconut
cream from the blending and swirl
it through on top. Softened cream
cheese would also work well.*

Ⓟ Swap out the silken tofu for
½ cup mashed pumpkin/sweet
potato/avocado/banana. I wouldn't
recommend applesauce, as it will be
too thin.

Layer desserts are great and
everything, but there is always one
part that beats out the others. With
tiramisu, it's the whipped layer in the
center, which puts the outer layers
to shame! Unlike traditional tiramisu,
which uses mascarpone cheese
and heavy cream, my version uses
a secret ingredient—silken tofu. I
promise you won't know it's in there.
For my paleo friends, you can swap it
for your favorite mashed starch.

In a high-speed blender or food processor,
combine all the ingredients and blend until
the desired consistency is achieved.

Transfer the tiramisu to a bowl or jar, top
with a sprinkle of cocoa powder, and enjoy!

MUG CAKES, COOKIES, AND MUFFINS

BAKERY STYLE FLOURLESS BLUEBERRY MUFFIN ⒼⓈ

YIELD

1 serving

COOKING TIME

Microwave 3 minutes,
Oven 12 to 15 minutes

NUTRITIONAL INFORMATION

Calories 210, Protein 12 grams,
Fat 3 grams, Fiber 5 grams

INGREDIENTS

½ cup gluten-free rolled oats

1 teaspoon baking powder

1 to 2 tablespoons granulated
sweetener of choice

2 tablespoons unsweetened
applesauce

2 tablespoons Greek yogurt
(dairy-free, if necessary)

1 large egg or egg white

2 tablespoons (or more) milk of
choice (dairy-free, if necessary)

1 to 2 tablespoons fresh or frozen
blueberries

1 teaspoon granulated sweetener of
choice, to sprinkle on top

*To make this recipe in the oven,
bake the muffin in a preheated oven
at 350 degrees Fahrenheit for 12 to
15 minutes, until it's tender on the
outside and a toothpick comes out
clean from the center.*

Ⓥ Sub out the egg/egg white for 1
tablespoon flax seeds (no need to
add extra liquid).

Grease a microwave-safe bowl or mug and set aside. Add all the ingredients, except for the blueberries, into a blender. Blend until fully processed. If the mixture is too thick, add a dash more milk of your choice until a thick batter is formed.

Transfer to the greased bowl or mug and stir in the blueberries. Top with the teaspoon of granulated sweetener and microwave for 60 to 90 seconds (depending on your microwave wattage), until the muffin is fully cooked through and fluffy on the inside.

I was never a huge fan of fruit in baked goods, with the exception of blueberry muffins. They were the only fruit-added bakery item I'd often choose over the others (even my beloved doughnuts and streusels). The key for it to be "bakery" style is an easy hack—simply sprinkle a teaspoon of your favorite granulated sweetener over the top before baking and *voilà*, the golden domes we adore!

CARAMEL APPLE
MUG CAKE ⓖⓟ

YIELD

1 serving

COOKING TIME

Microwave 3 minutes,
Oven 12 to 15 minutes

NUTRITIONAL INFORMATION

Calories 246, Protein 11 grams,
Fat 13 grams, Fiber 2 grams

INGREDIENTS

3 tablespoons almond meal

½ teaspoon baking powder

½ teaspoon cinnamon

¼ teaspoon sea salt

1 large egg

1 tablespoon pure maple syrup

1 teaspoon vanilla extract

2 tablespoons finely chopped fresh
apple pieces

1 teaspoon caramel sauce of choice

*To make this recipe in the oven,
bake the cake batter in an oven-safe
ramekin at 350 degrees Fahrenheit
for 12 to 15 minutes, until a toothpick
comes out clean.*

Ⓢ Use sugar-free maple syrup and
sugar-free caramel sauce, although
you may need to reduce the cooking
time slightly—sugar-free syrups tend
to dry out baked goods faster than
regular syrups. It would be best to
drizzle the cake in this instance.

I had big intentions of making
a caramel apple mug cake, which
involved caramel swirled through.
However, with various caramel
sauces on the market (paleo, sugar-
free, etc.), all having a different
effect, it was best to simply make
a small hole in the center and pour
in my caramel sauce of choice.
Alternatively, you can omit the hole
and drizzle the sauce over the top!

In a microwave-safe bowl, add the almond
meal, baking powder, cinnamon, and sea salt
and mix well.

In a separate bowl, combine the egg, maple
syrup, and vanilla and mix lightly. Pour
the egg mixture into the dry mixture. Add
the chopped apple pieces and mix well,
until combined. Scoop out a tablespoon of
the batter from the top and set aside. Pour a
tablespoon of caramel sauce into the center
and place the batter back on top. Microwave
for 60 to 90 seconds, until the cake is fluffy
and cooked through. Remove and enjoy!

DEEP DISH
SKILLET BROWNIE ⓖⓢⓥⓟ

YIELD

1 serving

COOKING TIME

10 to 12 minutes

NUTRITIONAL INFORMATION

Calories 253, Protein 8 grams,
Fat 23 grams, Fiber 8 grams

INGREDIENTS

2 tablespoons plus 2 teaspoons almond flour

1 tablespoon plus 2 teaspoons cocoa powder

½ teaspoon baking powder

1 tablespoon granulated sweetener of choice

1 tablespoon plus 1 teaspoon ground flax (can substitute with 1 large egg)

1 tablespoon oil of choice

2 tablespoons milk of choice

Chocolate chips, to top

This can be made in the microwave, however the texture can easily turn gummy if you overcook. Cook in 30-second intervals until your desired texture is achieved.

Ⓢ This works well with sugar-free chocolate chips.

Don't even think of looking at a boxed brownie mix: this skillet brownie has been my savior, and also my favorite dessert when the sweet tooth strikes. It uses easy on-hand ingredients and, as it doesn't contain any eggs, is perfect when just undercooked. Take it up a notch and add a scoop of ice cream!

Preheat the oven to 350 degrees Fahrenheit. Lightly grease a mini skillet or small baking dish or ramekin and set aside.

In a small mixing bowl, add the dry ingredients and mix well. Add in the oil and milk of choice and stir until a batter is formed. Top the batter with chocolate chips and bake in the preheated oven for 10 to 12 minutes, or until it's just cooked in the center and the chocolate chips have melted.

GIANT SHORTBREAD
COOKIE ⒼⓈⓋⓅ

YIELD

1 serving

COOKING TIME

10 to 13 minutes, plus time to firm up

NUTRITIONAL INFORMATION

Calories 222, Protein 12 grams,
Fat 17 grams, Fiber 3 grams

INGREDIENTS

2 tablespoons nut butter of choice

2 tablespoons granulated sweetener
of choice

1½ teaspoons coconut flour

1½ teaspoons egg whites

Chocolate chips of choice (optional)

*For a softer and chewier cookie,
remove from the oven after 10
minutes and allow it to cool on the
tray for 5 minutes.*

*For a shortbread-like cookie,
continue baking for up to 13 minutes.*

Ⓥ Omit the egg whites completely
and remove the cookie from the
oven at 8 to 9 minutes (soft and
chewy cookie) or 10 to 11 minutes
(shortbread consistency). If the
batter is too crumbly (not able to
form into a ball), add a dash of non-
dairy milk.

Shortbread doesn't need to be a
blend of pure butter and sugar. This
giant shortbread cookie crumbles
when you bite into it, but uses
wholesome ingredients to make!
For those who want a softer, chewier
cookie, it's easy to manipulate the
cooking time to fit the bill.

Preheat the oven to 350 degrees Fahrenheit.
Line a cookie sheet with baking paper and
set aside.

In a small mixing bowl, combine all the
ingredients and mix well.

Using your hands, form the batter into a
ball and transfer it to a greased cookie sheet.
Using a fork, press firmly into the batter to
form it into a cookie shape. Top with the
chocolate chips, if using.

Bake for 10 to 13 minutes, until the cookie is
just golden brown. Remove the cookie from
the oven and allow it to cool on a cookie sheet
to firm up.

GREEK YOGURT BLENDER CHOCOLATE MUFFIN ⒼⓈ

YIELD

1 serving

COOKING TIME

Microwave 5 minutes,
Oven 12 to 15 minutes

NUTRITIONAL INFORMATION

Calories 220, Protein 13 grams,
Fat 3 grams, Fiber 3 grams

INGREDIENTS

½ cup gluten-free rolled oats

1 teaspoon baking powder

1 tablespoon granulated sweetener
of choice

1 tablespoon cocoa powder

2 tablespoons unsweetened applesauce

2 tablespoons Greek yogurt
(dairy-free, if necessary)

1 large egg white

2 tablespoons milk of choice
(dairy-free, if necessary)

1 to 2 tablespoons chocolate chips,
as desired

*If you don't have access to a blender,
you can use gluten-free rolled oats
or another similar flour (such as
buckwheat) but reduce the amount
by a tablespoon and mix by hand.*

*If you opt for dairy-free yogurt, you'll
need less milk to form the batter, as
they are generally thin to begin with.
You can use all dairy-free yogurt and
omit the milk completely.*

*You can use a whole egg, but it will
be less fluffy.*

MICROWAVE OPTION:

Grease a microwave-safe bowl and set aside.
Add all the ingredients to a blender and blend
until fully immersed. If the mixture is too
thick, add a dash more milk of your choice.

Transfer the mixture to the greased bowl
and stir in the chocolate chips. Microwave
for 1 to 2 minutes, or until just cooked in the
center and fluffy.

OVEN OPTION:

Preheat the oven to 350 degrees Fahrenheit.

Follow the microwave directions but
transfer the mixture to a greased oven-safe
dish or ramekin. Bake for 10 to 12 minutes,
or until a toothpick comes out clean from
the center.

Using applesauce as a replacement for butter or margarine in baked goods was one of my first healthy hacks. Sometimes I found it to yield slightly drier baked goods. To combat this, I subbed out half the applesauce with yogurt and loved how fluffy they turned out! This blender chocolate muffin is proof of that.

This recipe is one of my favorites, because—depending on what kind of cookie you want—it's easily customizable. I love soft, chewy, and barely baked cookies and this fits the bill. If you want a chewier, firmer cookie, all you need to do is simply increase the cooking time. Also, it doesn't contain any eggs so if you want to barely bake it . . . go for it!

HALF~BAKED SKILLET
BREAKFAST COOKIE ⒢ⓥ

YIELD

1 serving

COOKING TIME

Microwave 5 minutes,
Oven 8 to 15 minutes

NUTRITIONAL INFORMATION

Calories 465, Protein 33 grams,
Fat 23 grams, Fiber 10 grams

INGREDIENTS

¼ cup gluten-free quick oats

2 tablespoons gluten-free oat flour

1 tablespoon cocoa powder

½ teaspoon baking powder

1 tablespoon ground flax

1 scoop vanilla protein powder
(32 to 34 grams, optional)

1 tablespoon coconut oil, melted
(or substitute with another neutral-
flavored oil, such as canola)

1 tablespoon pure maple syrup

¼ cup (or more) milk of choice
(dairy-free, if necessary)

1 to 2 tablespoons (or more)
chocolate chips

*To make this non-chocolate flavored,
leave out the cocoa powder and add
cinnamon/nutmeg/spices. Swap out
the chocolate chips for dried fruits/
mixed nuts, etc.*

*For a softer cookie, reduce the cooking
time—this recipe doesn't contain eggs
so it will be fine to enjoy under-baked.*

MICROWAVE OPTION:

In a microwave-safe bowl, add the dry ingredients and mix well.

Add in the melted coconut oil and maple
syrup and mix well until a crumbly batter
remains. Using a tablespoon, add your milk
of choice until a very thick batter is formed.
Stir in the chocolate chips, reserving a few
to add on top. Microwave for 2 to 3 minutes,
or until just cooked in the center.

OVEN OPTION:

Preheat the oven to 350 degrees Fahrenheit.
Lightly grease an oven-safe ramekin, mini
skillet, or small baking dish and set aside.

Follow the microwave instructions and
bake for 8 to 10 minutes, depending on the
power of your oven and the consistency you
want your deep-dish cookie to have.

⑤ This recipe works well with sugar-free syrup, as it
isn't used as the sole binder.

LOW-CARB TRIPLE CHOCOLATE MUG CAKE ⒼⓋⓅ

YIELD

1 serving

COOKING TIME

Microwave 5 minutes,
Oven 10 to 12 minutes

NUTRITIONAL INFORMATION

Calories 191, Protein 32 grams,
Fat 3 grams, Fiber 4 grams

INGREDIENTS

1 scoop protein powder
(32 to 34 grams)

½ teaspoon baking powder

1 tablespoon coconut flour

1 tablespoon granulated sweetener
of choice

1 large egg or ¼ cup liquid egg whites

¼ teaspoon vanilla extract

¼ cup (or more) milk of choice
(dairy-free, if necessary)

1 tablespoon mixed chocolate chips
(milk, dark, and white)

*If your protein powder is sweetened,
feel free to omit the granulated
sweetener of choice.*

Ⓢ Use sugar-free baking chips.

Ⓥ Omit the eggs completely—you
won't need any egg substitute either,
just add milk of choice until a thick
batter is formed.

MICROWAVE OPTION:

Add the dry ingredients to a greased, microwave-safe bowl. Mix until well combined.

Add the egg, vanilla extract, and your milk of choice and mix well, until a thick batter is formed. If the batter is too thick, add a little more milk. Top with chocolate chips and microwave for at least 60 seconds, and then in 10-second spurts until the cake is light and fluffy in the center.

OVEN OPTIONS:

Preheat the oven to 350 degrees Fahrenheit.

Follow the microwave directions but transfer the batter to a greased oven-safe dish or ramekin. Bake for 10 to 12 minutes, or until a toothpick comes out clean from the center.

Just because a recipe is deemed "low carb" does not mean it is "low flavor"—quite the opposite! As someone who loves working out, I try to refuel straight after. These mug cakes are great alternatives to protein shakes and they taste even better. The best bit? These can be batch-made and chucked in your gym bag to nosh on after those stretches!

MINI CONFETTI COOKIES ⒼⓋⓅ

YIELD

1 serving

COOKING TIME

8 to 12 minutes, plus time to firm up

NUTRITIONAL INFORMATION

Calories 400, Protein 34 grams,
Fat 20 grams, Fiber 11 grams

INGREDIENTS

1 scoop vanilla protein powder
(32 to 34 grams)

3 tablespoons coconut flour, sifted

¼ teaspoon sea salt

2 tablespoons cashew butter

1 tablespoon pure maple syrup

¼ teaspoon vanilla extract

1 to 2 tablespoons (or more) milk of
choice (dairy-free, if necessary)

Sprinkles

*For a softer, cake-like cookie, reduce
the cooking time. For firmer cookies,
cook until just golden brown and
allow the cookies to cool—they will
firm up quickly.*

Ⓢ Omit the maple syrup
completely—the cookies will still
turn out, albeit a little more crumbly
and firmer.

An entire batch of cookies that
you can eat in one sitting? Nope,
your eyes aren't deceiving you!
These secretly healthy cookies are
a cross between a cookie and a
cake, and perfect for breakfast or
a wholesome snack. For those who
want a crispier cookie, simply adjust
the cooking time.

Preheat the oven to 350 degrees Fahrenheit.
Line a cookie sheet or baking tray with
parchment paper and set it aside.

In a small mixing bowl, combine the
coconut flour, protein powder, and sea salt
and mix until no clumps remain.

In a small microwave-safe bowl or on the
stovetop, melt your nut butter and maple
syrup together. Whisk in the vanilla extract
and pour this mixture into the dry mixture.
Add your milk of choice a tablespoon at a
time until a thick batter is formed.

Using your hands, form the batter into small
balls and transfer them to the lined cookie
sheet. Press each ball into a cookie shape and
top with sprinkles. Bake for 8 to 12 minutes,
until the cookies turn just golden brown.

Remove the cookies from the oven and
allow them to cool before enjoying!

STRAWBERRIES AND CREAM MUG CAKE ⑥ⓥⓟ

YIELD

1 serving

COOKING TIME

Microwave 5 minutes,
Oven 12 to 15 minutes

NUTRITIONAL INFORMATION

Calories 288, Protein 9 grams,
Fat 16 grams, Fiber 6 grams

INGREDIENTS

2 tablespoons coconut flour

¼ teaspoon sea salt

¼ teaspoon baking powder

1 tablespoon neutral-flavored oil of choice (coconut or canola oil works great)

1 tablespoon plus 1 teaspoon pure maple syrup

¼ teaspoon vanilla extract

2 small eggs whites or 1 large egg (can substitute with 2 flax eggs, see page 26)

2 tablespoons milk of choice (dairy-free, if necessary)

2 to 3 strawberries, chopped

White chocolate chips/chunks, as desired

Fresh strawberries can be swapped out for frozen ones: simply thaw before adding into the cake, otherwise it will make the cake too moist. This also works with freeze-dried strawberries, but this will stain the cake red.

MICROWAVE OPTION:

Lightly grease a microwave-safe bowl or mug and set it aside.

In a small mixing bowl, add the dry ingredients and mix well. Add the wet ingredients to the dry—if the batter is crumbly, add a dash more milk of your choice. Stir in the chopped strawberries and top with white chocolate chips/chunks.

Microwave for 1 to 2 minutes, depending on your microwave power.

OVEN OPTION:

Preheat the oven to 350 degrees Fahrenheit and grease an oven-safe ramekin or baking dish with oil and set aside.

Follow microwave instructions and bake for 10 to 15 minutes, or until a toothpick comes out clean from the center.

❺ Add several pieces of chopped sugar-free white chocolate of choice, toward the end of cooking for easy melting. Also use sugar-free maple syrup, but increase by ½ a tablespoon.

ⓟ White cacao buttons work well for this, but only add them toward the end of baking, and chop them into smaller pieces.

White chocolate is the ugly duckling of chocolate—dark gets all the hype for being the better option, but in moderation white chocolate totally has its place. A small portion goes a very long way, especially when paired with the slightly tart strawberries. Another option is to switch out the strawberries for raspberries.

CLASSIC CHOCOLATE PROTEIN COOKIES ⒼⓈⓅ

YIELD

6 cookies

COOKING TIME

10 to 12 minutes, plus time to firm up

NUTRITIONAL INFORMATION

Calories 242, Protein 13 grams,
Fat 18 grams, Fiber 4 grams

INGREDIENTS

1 scoop chocolate protein powder
(32 to 34 grams)

¼ cup coconut flour

1 teaspoon baking powder

½ cup granulated sweetener of
choice (coconut palm sugar or brown
sugar works best)

1 large egg

1 teaspoon vanilla extract

¾ cup peanut butter (can substitute
with almond, cashew, or another
drippy nut butter)

¼ cup chocolate chunks (optional)

*If you use a non-peanut nut butter,
try to use a store-bought kind:
they tend to be more drippy than
homemade and cook much better.*

*If you don't have chocolate protein
powder, sub in vanilla and add a
tablespoon of cocoa powder. You
may need a dash of extra liquid (milk
or water) to form a dough.*

*Cookies can be kept in an airtight
container for up to a week. They can
be refrigerated for up to 2 weeks and
are freezer friendly.*

Preheat the oven to 350 degrees Fahrenheit. Line a cookie sheet or baking tray with parchment paper and set it aside.

In a large mixing bowl, combine the dry ingredients, mix, and set aside.

In a separate bowl, combine the egg, vanilla extract, and peanut butter and mix until the mixture is smooth and thick. Pour the egg mixture into the dry mixture and mix until they are fully incorporated. Stir through the chocolate chunks, if you choose.

Using your hands, form the dough into small, inch-thick balls and place them on the lined cookie sheet. Press down on each ball with a fork to form a cookie shape. Bake for 10 to 12 minutes, or until the cookies are just cooked on top. Remove the tray from the oven and allow the cookies to cool for 10 minutes before transferring them to a wire rack to cool completely.

Ⓢ Use a sugar-free baking blend as opposed to any sugar-free granulated sweetener.

Ⓥ Using a flax egg works only if you use peanut butter—I found it too difficult to hold when using almond or even cashew butter. It did work by leaving it out completely and using a little milk, but the cookies didn't come out crispy on the edges.

Check every single old-school peanut butter jar and they will all include the classic three-ingredient peanut butter cookie recipe. With a few sneaky changes, we can maintain the same flavor and texture, but on a healthier level!

I have a love affair with no-bake recipes, and cookies are no exception. What I love most about them is that, depending on whether you enjoy them at room temperature, from the fridge, or from the freezer, they all have different textures. My personal favorite is directly from the freezer—just let the cookie thaw slightly and dig in. It's like a firm fudge!

SOFT AND CHEWY NO-BAKE TRIPLE CHOCOLATE COOKIES ⒼⓋⓅ

YIELD

6 to 8 cookies, depending on size

COOKING TIME

10 minutes, plus 30 minutes minimum to firm up

NUTRITIONAL INFORMATION

Calories 329, Protein 13 grams, Fat 15 grams, Fiber 6 grams

INGREDIENTS

1½ cups oat flour

¼ cup coconut flour

⅛ teaspoon sea salt

1 scoop vanilla protein powder (32 to 34 grams)

½ cup smooth nut butter of choice

½ cup pure maple syrup

Milk of choice (dairy-free, if necessary), as needed

½ cup mixed chocolate chips (dark, white, or original)

Cookies are stable at room temperature, but best kept refrigerated for the ultimate fudgy texture.

Protein powder isn't necessary. If you do omit it, you'll need less of your milk of choice to create the batter.

Ⓢ Use sugar-free chocolate chips. Use sugar-free maple syrup, increasing the amount by an extra ¼ cup.

Ⓟ Swap the oat flour for almond flour or ½ cup of coconut flour (in addition to the coconut flour already in the recipe).

Line a large baking tray or plate with parchment paper and set it aside.

In a large mixing bowl, combine the flours, protein powder (if using), and sea salt, and mix well.

In a microwave-safe bowl or on the stovetop, melt your nut butter with maple syrup until they are combined. Pour the syrup mixture into the dry mixture and mix until well combined—the batter should be very crumbly.

Using a tablespoon at a time, add your milk of choice and mix until a thick batter is formed. Stir in the chocolate chips until fully incorporated. Using your hands, form the batter into small balls and place them on the lined baking tray or plate.

Press each ball firmly into a cookie shape and refrigerate for 30 minutes, or until they are firm.

THREE~INGREDIENT PEANUT BUTTER FUDGE GVP

YIELD

6 to 8 servings

COOKING TIME

10 minutes, plus time to firm up

NUTRITIONAL INFORMATION

Calories 263, Protein 7 grams,
Fat 23 grams, Fiber 2 grams

INGREDIENTS

¼ cup coconut oil

1 cup smooth peanut butter

2 tablespoons maple syrup

P Swap out the peanut butter for almond, cashew, or sunflower seed butter

How do you know if a healthier fudge gets the seal of approval? Get your grandma to taste test it! My grandma makes the best fudge, but like most traditional versions, hers is based on condensed milk, butter, and sugar. While this fudge contains none of those, it's still creamy, smooth, and melts in your mouth.

Line a 12-count mini muffin tray with muffin liners and set it aside.

Melt your peanut butter with your coconut oil in a microwave-safe bowl or on the stovetop. Stir in the maple syrup and mix until fully incorporated.

Divide the mixture evenly amongst the mini muffin slots and refrigerate or freeze them until they are firm, around 2 hours.

This recipe has been made by thousands of readers and is a favorite because of how easy it is and the minimal ingredient list. While not true-blue brownies, they have a delicious fudgy texture that satisfies any chocolate craving! The recipe is also easily adaptable and can be customized to whichever nut butter or mashed starch you have on hand!

THREE-INGREDIENT FLOURLESS PUMPKIN BROWNIES ⑤⑤♥℗

YIELD

6 brownies

COOKING TIME

15 to 20 minutes

NUTRITIONAL INFORMATION

Calories 143, Protein 6 grams,
Fat 11 grams, Fiber 4 grams

INGREDIENTS

1 cup pumpkin puree

½ cup nut butter of choice

¼ cup (or more) cocoa powder

These brownies are not sweet and are more on the rich and dark side. If you prefer a sweeter brownie, top them with your favorite frosting.

For gooey brownies, remove the brownies from the oven when they seem a little underdone—the brownies will firm up once cooled.

You can easily swap out the pumpkin for banana or sweet potato. Please note, the banana is a little overpowering and its flavor is very evident.

Preheat the oven to 350 degrees Fahrenheit. Coat an 8 × 4-inch loaf pan with cooking spray and set it aside.

Add all the ingredients to a high-speed blender or a large mixing bowl and mix very well, until the ingredients are fully combined and a thick batter remains.

Transfer the brownie batter to the loaf pan and bake for 15 to 20 minutes, or until a toothpick comes out "just" clean from the center. Allow the brownies to cool in the pan completely before frosting or slicing into bars.

FOUR-INGREDIENT FLOURLESS BROWNIES ⑥Ⓢ♥Ⓟ

YIELD

4 brownies

COOKING TIME

12 to 15 minutes, depending on texture desired

NUTRITIONAL INFORMATION

Calories 255, Protein 15 grams, Fat 17 grams, Fiber 7 grams

INGREDIENTS

1 scoop chocolate protein powder (32 to 34 grams)

1 cup mashed starch of choice (banana, pumpkin, or sweet potato)

¼ cup cocoa powder

½ cup smooth nut butter of choice (peanut butter, almond butter, or cashew butter)

These brownies aren't super sweet— I don't recommend adding sweetener to the batter, but rather that you drizzle some chocolate or healthy frosting over the top.

If you don't like the taste of banana, use pumpkin or sweet potato as the starch base.

For a richer chocolate taste, feel free to increase the cocoa powder. Blend a little longer to ensure it is dispersed in the batter.

If you don't have a blender/food processor, you can easily mix it all by hand, although there may be small clumps.

Hands down, these brownies are the most frequently made and most popular recipe on my site. It's hard to come across a protein-packed sweet treat that doesn't include multiple egg whites and a slew of artificial sweeteners, or a recipe that doesn't come out dry as a hockey puck! These brownies are super fudgy and take less than 20 minutes to whip up.

Preheat the oven to 350 degrees Fahrenheit. Cover an 8 × 4-inch loaf pan with tin foil and grease it lightly.

In a high-speed blender or food processor, add all the ingredients and blend until a smooth batter remains.

Pour the batter in the lined loaf pan and bake for 12 to 15 minutes, until a toothpick comes out clean. Allow the brownies to cool in the pan completely before slicing.

NO-BAKE
RECIPES

When I put a call out for recipe requests on my blog, there was an overwhelming request for all things cake batter. I wanted to share something unique and true to its name, so what better than something that resembles cake batter? This "dip" is thick, creamy, and can be customized to suit your taste buds. It can be prepped in advance and even used as a pre- or post-workout snack!

CAKE BATTER DIP FOR ONE ⒼⓋⓅ

YIELD

1 serving

COOKING TIME

5 minutes, plus 30 minutes to chill

NUTRITIONAL INFORMATION

Calories 424, Protein 34 grams,
Fat 18 grams, Fiber 7 grams

INGREDIENTS

2 tablespoons gluten-free oat flour

1 to 2 tablespoons granulated sweetener of choice

¼ teaspoon sea salt

1 scoop vanilla protein powder (32 to 34 grams)

½ cup unsweetened applesauce (can substitute with mashed banana, sweet potato, or pumpkin)

2 tablespoons smooth peanut, almond, or cashew butter, etc.

1 tablespoon maple syrup

½ teaspoon vanilla extract

Milk of choice, as needed

Ⓢ Use sugar-free maple syrup.

Ⓟ Substitute the oat flour with 1 tablespoon of coconut flour.

In a large mixing bowl, combine the flour, sweetener of choice, sea salt, and protein powder, and mix well. Add your mashed starch of choice and mix until fully incorporated. The mixture should be extremely crumbly.

In a microwave-safe bowl or on the stovetop, melt your nut butter with the maple syrup, and whisk through the vanilla extract. Pour the nut butter mixture into the mixing bowl and stir until everything is fully combined. Add your milk of choice a tablespoon at a time until a thick cake-like batter is formed. Transfer to a bowl and refrigerate for 30 minutes, until the batter has thickened. Top with optional sprinkles and enjoy!

Feel free to omit the granulated sweetener, especially if your protein powder is sweetened. Alternatively, if it's not sweet enough, feel free to add an extra tablespoon or two.

I prefer using applesauce as it's the mildest tasting. If you use pumpkin or sweet potato, you may need to add more sweetener of your choice to mask the taste.

Depending on the flour you use, you may need more milk of your choice to reach the desired consistency.

EDIBLE **COOKIE DOUGH** Ⓖⓥⓟ

YIELD

1 serving

COOKING TIME

10 minutes, plus more if refrigerated

NUTRITIONAL INFORMATION

Calories 442, Protein 35 grams,
Fat 22 grams, Fiber 13 grams

INGREDIENTS

¼ cup coconut flour (can substitute
with almond, peanut, or gluten-free
oat flour)

1 scoop vanilla protein powder
(32 to 34 grams, optional)

¼ teaspoon sea salt

2 tablespoons nut butter of choice

1 tablespoon maple syrup

¼ cup (or more) milk of choice
(dairy-free, if necessary)

Chocolate chips/trail mix/etc., to top

*Depending on the flours/protein
powder you use, you may need more
milk of your choice to thicken the
dough.*

*This tastes delicious when
refrigerated for a few hours before,
as it thickens up nicely like a batter.*

*If you don't use protein powder or if
the one you choose is unsweetened,
feel free to add 1 to 2 tablespoons of
a sweetener of your choice.*

Ⓢ Swap out the maple syrup for
sugar-free syrup or 1 tablespoon of
granulated sugar-free sweetener of
choice.

There was a good reason my mum banned me from helping her in the kitchen as a kid: half the cookie dough wouldn't even make it into the oven! If only that cookie dough was as healthy as this recipe was, she'd probably have reconsidered. This edible cookie dough is smooth, creamy, and can be as thick or smooth as you want—it doesn't discriminate!

In a small mixing bowl, add the dry ingredients and set them aside.

In a microwave-safe bowl or on the stovetop, melt your nut butter with the maple syrup until they are combined. Pour the nut butter mixture into the dry mixture and mix until a crumbly batter remains.

Add your milk of choice a tablespoon at a time until a cookie dough remains. Enjoy immediately or refrigerate to thicken up.

LEMON POPPY SEED PROTEIN BARS Ⓖ Ⓥ Ⓟ

YIELD

4 bars

COOKING TIME

15 minutes, plus 30 minutes to firm up

NUTRITIONAL INFORMATION

Calories 147, Protein 8 grams, Fat 7 grams, Fiber 4 grams

INGREDIENTS

½ cup gluten-free oat flour

2 tablespoons coconut flour

1 to 2 tablespoons granulated sweetener of choice (optional)

¼ teaspoon sea salt

½ scoop protein powder (16 to 17 grams, optional)

1½ teaspoons poppy seeds

1 teaspoon lemon zest (optional)

2 tablespoons nut butter of choice

3 tablespoons pure maple syrup

½ teaspoon lemon extract

2 tablespoons (or more) milk of choice (dairy-free, if necessary)

White chocolate chips, to drizzle (optional)

I omitted any granulated sweetener as I found the bars sweet enough, thanks to the protein powder. Adjust according to your taste.

In a large mixing bowl, combine the dry ingredients and set them aside.

In a microwave-safe bowl or on the stovetop, melt your nut butter together with the maple syrup. Lightly whisk in the lemon extract and pour the nut butter mixture into the dry mixture. Mix until a thick, crumbly texture remains. Add your milk of choice a tablespoon at a time, until a very thick batter is formed.

Transfer the protein bar mixture into a 4-inch square or mini loaf pan lined with parchment paper and refrigerate for 30 minutes or so, until firm. Once firm, top with the optional white chocolate drizzle, cut it into bars, and enjoy!

Ⓢ Swap out the maple syrup for sugar-free maple syrup, but do not melt it with the nut butter—it won't turn out well. Simply stir it in the batter once you're ready to form the bars. If the batter is too drippy, add a dash more coconut flour to firm it up. You can also omit the syrup completely and increase the milk of your choice; however, bars will be more crumbly and less sweet.

Ⓟ Swap out the oat flour for fine-milled almond flour. You may need to increase the milk of your choice to compensate.

Pucker up—your post-workout snack just got that much better! These small-batch protein bars beat out anything on the market. They use fewer ingredients and have a hint of lemon, which reminds you of a lemon bar. They also have perfect texture, even out of the freezer!

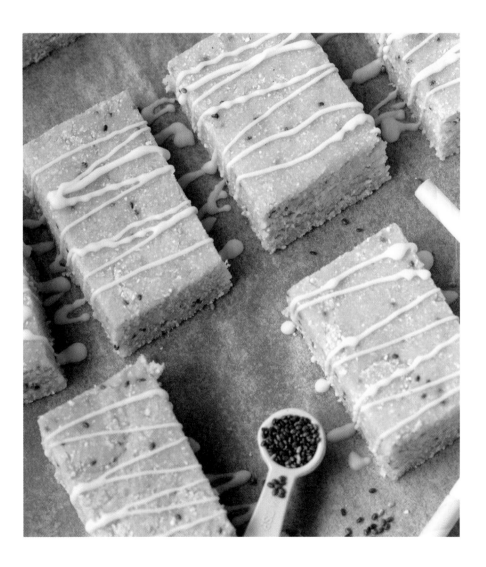

Pumpkin isn't just reserved for fall—it makes a fantastic addition to many sweet recipes and works as a fantastic binder! These no-bake soft-baked cookies are deceptively filling and have a fudge-like texture. They can also be batch-made and frozen in individual portions for grab-and-go breakfasts.

NO~BAKE SOFT BAKED PUMPKIN COOKIE ⓖⓥⓟ

YIELD

1 serving

COOKING TIME

5 minutes, plus time to firm up

NUTRITIONAL INFORMATION

Calories 376, Protein 34 grams,
Fat 15 grams, Fiber 13 grams

INGREDIENTS

3 tablespoons coconut flour

1 tablespoon almond flour
(can substitute with a teaspoon
of coconut flour)

2 tablespoons granulated sweetener
of choice

¼ teaspoon cinnamon

¼ teaspoon sea salt

1 scoop vanilla protein powder of
choice (32 to 34 grams, optional)

2 tablespoons pure maple syrup

1 tablespoon nut butter of choice

¼ cup pumpkin puree

Milk of choice, as needed

*I omitted any granulated sweetener
as I found the cookie sweet enough,
thanks to the protein powder. Adjust
according to your taste.*

*If you don't have pumpkin, feel free
to substitute with mashed sweet
potato or applesauce.*

In a large mixing bowl, combine the dry ingredients and set aside.

In a microwave-safe bowl or on the stovetop, melt your nut butter together with the maple syrup. Transfer the nut butter mixture to the dry mixture and add the pumpkin puree. Mix until a thick, crumbly texture remains. Add your milk of choice a tablespoon at a time, until a very thick batter is formed.

Form the batter into a ball, transfer it to a plate, and press it into a large cookie shape. Drizzle the cookie with coconut butter, if desired.

Ⓢ Swap out the maple syrup for sugar-free maple syrup, but do not melt with the nut butter—it won't turn out well. Simply stir it in the batter instead. If the batter is too drippy, add a dash more coconut flour to firm it up. You can also omit the syrup completely and increase the milk of your choice; however, the soft-baked cookie will be more crumbly and less sweet.

NO~BAKE GRANOLA BAR COOKIE ⑤Ⓥ

YIELD

1 serving

COOKING TIME

10 minutes, plus time to firm up

NUTRITIONAL INFORMATION

Calories 500, Protein 37 grams,
Fat 22 grams, Fiber 10 grams

INGREDIENTS

½ cup gluten-free rolled oats

1 tablespoon coconut flour
(or substitute with an extra
tablespoon of rolled oats)

¼ teaspoon cinnamon

¼ teaspoon sea salt

1 scoop vanilla protein powder of
choice (32 to 34 grams)

2 tablespoons nut butter of choice

1 tablespoon brown rice syrup
(or substitute with agave, honey,
or maple syrup)

¼ cup (or more) milk of choice
(dairy-free, if necessary)

1 to 2 tablespoons chocolate chips of
choice (optional)

*I omitted any granulated sweetener
as I found the cookie sweet enough,
thanks to the protein powder. Adjust
according to your taste.*

*If you use agave, honey, or maple
syrup, you may want to add an extra
teaspoon, as they are not as sticky as
brown rice syrup.*

Line a large plate with parchment paper and set it aside.

Combine the rolled oats, coconut flour, cinnamon, sea salt, and vanilla protein powder in a large mixing bowl. Stir the mixture and set it aside.

In a microwave-safe bowl or on the stovetop, melt your nut butter together with the brown rice syrup until they are combined. Pour the nut butter mixture into the dry mixture and mix until a crumbly texture remains. Add your milk of choice, adding an extra tablespoon or more if the batter is not thick enough. Form the batter into a large ball and transfer it to the lined plate. Press the batter into a cookie shape and top with chocolate chips, if using.

Refrigerate for 30 minutes or more, to firm up.

⑤ Swap out the maple syrup for sugar-free maple syrup, but do not melt it with the nut butter—it won't turn out well. Simply stir it in the batter instead. If the batter is too drippy, add a dash more coconut flour or rolled oats to firm it up. You can also omit the syrup completely and increase the milk of your choice; however, the granola bar cookie will be more crumbly and less sweet.

Store-bought granola bars are infamously deceptive: you think you'll be enjoying a healthy snack but in actual fact they are worse for you than some candy bars! Not only that, there isn't too much variety. This single-serve granola bar cookie is perfect to satisfy hunger, either for breakfast or a wholesome snack. It holds up really well and doesn't need any refrigeration once firm.

RICE CRISPY TREATS ⑤Ⓥ

YIELD

1 serving

COOKING TIME

10 minutes, plus 30 minutes
to firm up

NUTRITIONAL INFORMATION

Calories 363, Protein 15 grams,
Fat 17 grams, Fiber 3 grams

INGREDIENTS

½ cup gluten-free crispy rice cereal
of choice

2 tablespoons protein powder
(optional)

2 tablespoons nut butter of choice

1 tablespoon brown rice syrup
(or substitute with maple syrup)

Chocolate, to drizzle (optional)

*I prefer brown rice syrup, as it is
much stickier than maple syrup and
holds the rice crispy treat together
better. If you use maple syrup, you
may consider increasing the amount
by a teaspoon or two to ensure the
treat does not fall apart.*

*If you have difficulty forming the rice
crispy into a bar or ball shape, lightly
wet your hands prior to doing so.*

Ⓢ Sugar-free maple syrup will not
work for this—it simply does not have
the natural stickiness necessary.
You can use a milk of your choice to
help form the bar, but you'd need to
freeze the rice crispy treat or enjoy
it immediately to avoid it becoming
soggy.

Can we throw back to our childhood lunch box for a second? Rice crispy treats were a staple, and the one snack that people would trade their whole brown bag for. While traditional rice crispy treats rely on marshmallows and butter to hold together, this one uses nut butter and brown rice syrup, with an additional boost of protein powder.

Line a small plate with parchment paper and set it aside.

In a small bowl, combine the crispy rice cereal with protein powder and mix until combined.

In a microwave-safe bowl or on the stovetop, melt your nut butter together with the brown rice syrup. Pour the nut butter mixture over the dry mixture and gently stir until fully combined.

Using your hands, form the rice crispy into a ball or bar shape and transfer it to the lined plate. Drizzle it with chocolate and refrigerate for 30 minutes, or until it's firm.

HEALTHY NO~BAKE VANILLA BREAKFAST BLONDIES ⓖⓥ

YIELD

8 large pieces

COOKING TIME:

10 minutes, plus 30 minutes to firm up

NUTRITIONAL INFORMATION:

Calories 270, Protein 15 grams, Fat 11 grams, Fiber 6 grams

FOR THE BLONDIES

1½ cups gluten-free oat flour

¼ cup coconut flour

¼ teaspoon cinnamon

2 scoops protein powder (64 to 67 grams, optional)

2 tablespoons granulated sweetener of choice

½ teaspoon vanilla extract

½ cup almond butter (can substitute with any nut or nut-free alternative)

½ cup brown rice syrup (can substitute with honey or pure maple syrup)

1 tablespoon (or more) milk of choice

FOR THE PROTEIN FROSTING

2 scoops vanilla protein powder (64 to 67 grams)

1 to 2 tablespoons granulated sweetener of choice

1 tablespoon (or more) milk of choice

FOR THE COCONUT BUTTER FROSTING

¼ cup coconut butter, softened

Line an 8-inch square baking pan with parchment paper and set aside.

In a large mixing bowl, combine the flours, protein powder, cinnamon, and granulated sweetener, and set aside.

In a microwave-safe bowl or on the stovetop, melt the almond butter together with the brown rice syrup until combined. Whisk in the vanilla extract and pour the almond butter mixture into the dry mixture. Mix well until a crumbly texture remains. Add your milk of choice, one tablespoon at a time, until a very thick batter remains. Pour batter into the lined baking pan and press firmly in place.

Refrigerate for at least 30 minutes, or until firm. Add your frosting of choice and refrigerate slightly to firm up. Cut into bars and enjoy!

Depending on the protein powder you use, you may need more of your milk of choice. If batter is too thin, add more coconut flour to firm up.

Ⓢ You can use sugar-free maple syrup, but don't melt the syrup with the nut butter, just ensure the nut butter is softened. You won't need as much milk of choice to firm up.

Ⓟ Swap out the oat flour for almond flour.

... And the dessert for breakfast theme continues! I love these vanilla breakfast blondies because depending on how you store them, they have a different texture. For thick, chewy bars, keep them refrigerated and eat as is. For soft, fudge-like bars, let them thaw at room temperature for about 30 minutes.

HEALTHY NO-BAKE CHOCOLATE CHIP PROTEIN COOKIES ⒼⓋ

YIELD

10 cookies

COOKING TIME:

10 minutes, plus time to firm up

NUTRITIONAL INFORMATION:

Calories 186, Protein 9 grams, Fat 7 grams, Fiber 4 grams

INGREDIENTS:

1½ cups gluten-free oat flour

¼ cup coconut flour

1 scoop vanilla protein powder (32 to 33 grams)

¼ cup plus 2 tablespoons nut butter of choice (peanut, almond, cashew, sunflower seed)

⅓ cup pure maple syrup

1 teaspoon vanilla extract

¼ cup (or more) milk of choice

Chocolate chips of choice

Ⓢ You can omit the syrup completely, but add some granulated sweetener of choice.

Ⓟ Swap out the oat flour for almond flour.

When your cookies can pass as a post-workout snack, that is the motivation you need to hit the gym! These foolproof cookies are soft, chewy, and can be rolled into balls or bars—they are super customizable.

In a large mixing bowl, combine your dry ingredients and set aside.

In a microwave-safe bowl or on the stovetop, melt your nut butter together with the maple syrup until combined. Stir in the vanilla extract and pour the nut butter mixture into the dry mixture. Add your milk of choice, one tablespoon at a time, until a very thick batter is formed.

Using your hands, form into small balls, and place on a lined plate. Press each ball into a cookie shape and add chocolate chips, if using, on top. Refrigerate for at least 20 minutes to firm up.

SMALL
BATCH
SNACKS

CHUNKY MONKEY PROTEIN TRAIL MIX ⓒⓢⓥⓟ

YIELD

2 to 4 servings

COOKING TIME

15 minutes, plus time to cool completely

NUTRITIONAL INFORMATION

Calories 265, Protein 12 grams, Fat 18 grams, Fiber 5 grams

INGREDIENTS

3 tablespoons granulated sweetener of choice

¼ teaspoon cinnamon

1 tablespoon water

¼ teaspoon vanilla extract

¾ cup raw, unsalted almonds

1 scoop protein powder (32 to 34 grams)

¼ cup banana chips

¼ cup chocolate buttons

Feel free to substitute the almonds with any kind of nut.

Chunky Monkey Protein Trail Mix can be kept in an airtight container for up to 2 weeks.

If you'd like to make clusters, increase the granulated sweetener by an extra tablespoon and increase the water by a teaspoon. Once the mix has been removed from the heat and the protein has been stirred in, allow it to sit for 10 minutes before breaking into clusters.

Heat a large frying pan or deep pot over medium heat. When it's hot, add the granulated sweetener of choice, cinnamon, water, and vanilla extract and mix well. Allow the mixture to heat up, stirring occasionally.

When the sweetener has completely melted, add the almonds and mix until they are fully incorporated. Watch over the pan and continue stirring often until most of the sugar has been coated and begins to crystallize. Continue stirring until the mixture begins to lose moisture.

Remove the mixture from the pan and allow it to sit for 1 to 2 minutes. Stir through the protein powder and mix until the almonds are fully coated. Transfer the trail mix to a baking tray to cool completely. Once the trail mix cool, add the banana chips and chocolate buttons and stir.

I love trail mix—it's convenient, it's portable, and it's relatively filling . . . but only if you add a boost of protein into it! This sneaky hack is an easy way to add protein to it, and no oven is needed— you can make it on the stovetop. It's also extremely customizable, so throw in your favorite trail mix add-ins or switch up the nuts.

CUSTOMIZABLE PROTEIN POPCORN ⓖⓢⓥ

YIELD

2 servings

COOKING TIME

5 minutes

NUTRITIONAL INFORMATION

Calories 275, Protein 29 grams,
Fat 3 grams, Fiber 7 grams

INGREDIENTS

1 scoop vanilla protein powder
(32 to 34 grams)

¼ teaspoon sea salt

2 tablespoons granulated sweetener
of choice

5 to 6 cups air-popped popcorn

Cooking oil spray

½ cup add-ins of choice (candy
pieces, nuts, dried fruit, seeds, etc.)

*You can omit the protein powder
and give it a savory twist by adding
nutritional yeast or peanut flour.*

*Popcorn can be stored at room
temperature for up to 3 days*

Movie time just got that much better. I think snacking in front of the big screen is one of the highlights of going to the cinema. Saying that, we'll be swapping the usual butter- and sugar-laden popcorn for one that is air popped and with a sneaky protein twist. For a bit of fun, throw in half a cup of your favorite sweet or savory bits.

In a small mixing bowl, combine the protein powder, sea salt, and sweetener of choice and mix well.

In a large mixing bowl, add the popcorn, lightly spray it with cooking spray, and gently stir to ensure most of the popcorn is covered. Pour the protein powder mixture over the popcorn and shake very well, until the popcorn is coated. Add your toppings of choice and enjoy!

PALEO GRANOLA ⓖⓥⓟ

YIELD

2 to 3 servings

COOKING TIME

12 to 15 minutes, plus time to cool completely

NUTRITIONAL INFORMATION

Calories 242, Protein 7 grams, Fat 20 grams, Fiber 4 grams

INGREDIENTS

1 cup unsweetened coconut flakes

½ cup sliced almonds

1 tablespoon chia seeds

⅓ cup pumpkin seeds

⅓ cup sunflower seeds

1 teaspoon cinnamon

1 tablespoon oil of choice (I prefer coconut or safflower)

3 tablespoons pure maple syrup

Dried fruit/chocolate chunks (optional)

Do not substitute the maple syrup with sugar-free syrup—it won't work.

This granola is not overly sweet. It works great as a topping for yogurt or as a trail mix.

Think granola has to be chock-full of grains? Think again! For those following a grain-free diet, this small batch granola is your answer. It's perfect when mixed with your favorite fruit and nuts as a trail mix or, my personal favorite, as a yogurt topping!

Preheat the oven to 350 degrees Fahrenheit. Line a large baking tray with parchment paper and set it aside.

In a large mixing bowl, add all the ingredients except for the oil, maple syrup, and optional fruit or chocolate chunks. Mix well. In a microwave-safe bowl or on the stovetop, melt your oil and syrup together. Pour the syrup mixture into the dry mixture and stir until the granola is fully coated.

Spread the granola mixture in a single layer on the lined baking tray and bake for 12 to 15 minutes, stirring halfway through to avoid burning.

Allow the granola to cool completely before stirring through the dried fruits and chocolate chips and storing in an airtight container for up to 4 weeks.

PEANUT BUTTER CUP
CEREAL POPS Ⓖ Ⓥ

YIELD

2 servings

COOKING TIME

10 to 15 minutes, plus time to firm up

NUTRITIONAL INFORMATION

Calories 383, Protein 24 grams,
Fat 21 grams, Fiber 9 grams

INGREDIENTS

¼ cup peanut flour (or substitute with protein powder)

1 tablespoon coconut flour

2 tablespoons peanut butter

1 tablespoon pure maple syrup

Milk of choice, as needed

1 tablespoon chocolate chips of choice

1 tablespoon chopped peanuts

The smaller the balls are, the faster they will bake. Keep an eye on them!

Do-it-yourself cereal is easier than you think. These cereal pops are ridiculously versatile: you can mix it through yogurt, enjoy it as a trail mix, or make it in a big batch as it keeps beautifully!

Preheat the oven to 350 degrees Fahrenheit. Line a large baking tray or cookie sheet with parchment paper and set it aside.

In a small mixing bowl, add the peanut flour (or protein powder) and coconut flour and mix until combined. Stir through your peanut butter and maple syrup until a crumbly texture remains. Add your milk of choice, one tablespoon at a time, until a very thick batter is formed.

Using your hands, form bite-size balls and set them on the lined baking tray. Bake for 10 to 15 minutes, or until they are just golden brown on top. Do not over-bake, as they burn easily.

FOUR-INGREDIENT CASHEW BUTTER FREEZER FUDGE ⒼⓋⓅ

YIELD

8 pieces

COOKING TIME

10 minutes, plus time to firm up

NUTRITIONAL INFORMATION

Calories 106, Protein 6 grams,
Fat 8 grams, Fiber 1 gram

INGREDIENTS

½ cup cashew butter

¼ cup protein powder (or substitute
with peanut flour)

2 tablespoons maple syrup

1 tablespoon (or more) milk of choice
(dairy-free, if necessary)

*Sometimes the protein powder can
be a little gritty—if this is the case,
continue to add milk or liquid until
it's smooth.*

*The fudge needs to be stored in the
freezer—it only takes 5 minutes to
thaw out.*

*Feel free to add cocoa powder to
make it chocolate flavored.*

Ⓢ Use sugar-free maple syrup.

Line a mini loaf pan with parchment paper. Spray the dish lightly with cooking spray and set it aside.

In a microwave-safe bowl or on the stovetop, melt your cashew butter. Gently stir in the protein powder until it's fully incorporated. Add the maple syrup and continue mixing until everything is combined. If the mixture is too crumbly, add your milk of choice a tablespoon at a time.

Pour the fudge mixture into the lined baking dish and freeze it for 30 minutes, or until it's firm. Remove the fudge and cut it into pieces. Store the pieces in the freezer and simply thaw them for 5 minutes before consuming.

A twist on the classic fudge, this version includes a boost of protein. And because it's designed to be enjoyed frozen, it requires no coconut oil! It's a quick and easy protein-packed sweet treat to satisfy the cravings.

A serving of vegetables in these espresso bars? You bet! Once again, the humble sweet potato gets mashed and blended and disguised in another recipe. It's fudgy, rich, and has the perfect texture. Enjoy one straight from the fridge for the ultimate snack.

SECRET INGREDIENT
ESPRESSO FUDGE BARS ⒼⓋⓅ

YIELD

4 large bars

COOKING TIME

15 to 20 minutes, plus time to cool completely

NUTRITIONAL INFORMATION (INCLUDING PROTEIN FROSTING)

Calories 325, Protein 21 grams, Fat 17 grams, Fiber 6 grams

INGREDIENTS

½ cup smooth nut butter of choice

2 tablespoons maple syrup

1 cup mashed sweet potato

¼ cup cocoa powder

1 teaspoon espresso powder

¼ cup chocolate chips (optional)

PROTEIN FROSTING

2 scoops chocolate protein powder

2 tablespoons maple syrup

Milk of your choice, as needed (dairy-free, if necessary)

BASIC FROSTING

10 ounces baking chips, melted

These fudge bars may seem undercooked when first removed from the oven, but they will firm up slightly.

The bars should be kept refrigerated, and can be stored for up to 7 days. They are freezer friendly too, and can be stored for up to 2 months for optimum freshness.

Preheat the oven to 350 degrees Fahrenheit. Cover an 8 × 4-inch loaf pan with aluminum foil, then lightly grease and set it aside.

In a small microwave-safe bowl or on the stovetop, melt your nut butter together with the maple syrup. In a large mixing bowl, add the mashed sweet potato, melted nut butter mixture, cocoa powder, and espresso powder and mix well. If you're using chocolate chips, stir them in.

Pour the mixture into the greased pan and bake for 15 to 20 minutes, or until it's just cooked through. Remove the pan from the oven and allow the fudge to cool in the pan completely.

While the bars are cooling, make the protein frosting. In a small bowl, combine the protein powder with the maple syrup and your milk of choice until a thick frosting-like consistency remains.

Top the cooled fudge bars with the protein frosting or pour over melted chocolate and refrigerate until the bars are firm.

Ⓢ Omit the maple syrup and add a milk of your choice instead, along with 1 to 2 tablespoons granulated sweetener of your choice. Do not over-bake these, or they will come out too crumbly.

BLENDER CHOCOLATE MUFFINS ⓖⓢⓥ

YIELD

10 to 12 muffins

COOKING TIME

20 to 30 minutes, plus cooling time

**NUTRITIONAL INFORMATION
(INCLUDING PROTEIN FROSTING)**

Calories 141, Protein 9 grams,
Fat 7 grams, Fiber 3 grams

INGREDIENTS

2¼ cups gluten-free rolled oats

2 tablespoons cocoa powder

½ cup granulated sweetener of choice

1 tablespoon baking powder

¼ teaspoon sea salt

1 cup pureed sweet potato
(or substitute with banana, pumpkin,
or applesauce)

1 cup milk of choice (dairy-free, if
necessary)

1 large egg (or substitute with
1 flax egg)

1 teaspoon vanilla extract

6 tablespoons nut butter of choice

PROTEIN FROSTING

2 scoops chocolate protein powder
(64 to 68 grams)

Milk of choice, at room temperature

1 tablespoon coconut oil, melted

*These muffins are freezer friendly. I
love wrapping each up individually
for perfectly portioned snacks.*

Preheat the oven to 350 degrees Fahrenheit. Grease a 12-count muffin tin, line it with muffin liners, and set it aside.

Add all the muffin ingredients to a high-speed blender and blend until they are well combined. Alternatively, you can use a food processor or mix by hand.

Pour the batter into each muffin tin, approximately three-quarters full. Bake for 20 to 30 minutes, or until a toothpick comes out clean. Remove the tin from the oven and allow the muffins to cool in the tin for 10 minutes before transferring the muffins to a wire rack to cool completely.

In a small bowl, mix the chocolate with your milk of choice and coconut oil until a thick frosting is formed. Once the muffins are completely cooled, top with the frosting.

You can have fluffy, bakery-style muffins made without butter or oil: the key here is using a mashed starch to retain moisture and texture. These muffins are one of my favorites, as it's a no-mess recipe. Just throw everything in a blender and transfer to the muffin tins to bake. The protein frosting tastes like the real deal!

This recipe goes way back to my first foray into fitness— I despised protein shakes and instead would enjoy these blondies post-workout. I revamped this recipe to make a small batch—so small, you can enjoy the entire serving! The frosting is optional, but offers an even bigger dose of protein.

FROSTED BLONDIES ⑤⑤

YIELD

4 blondies

COOKING TIME

12 to 15 minutes, plus time to cool
completely

**NUTRITIONAL INFORMATION
(INCLUDING FROSTING)**

Calories 210, Protein 14 grams,
Fat 11 grams, Fiber 3 grams

INGREDIENTS

½ cup gluten-free oat flour
(can substitute with gluten-free
whole wheat)

½ scoop vanilla protein powder
(16 to 17 grams)

¼ cup granulated sweetener of choice

½ teaspoon baking powder

¼ teaspoon baking soda

¼ teaspoon sea salt

1 large egg

¼ teaspoon vanilla extract

¼ cup milk of choice (dairy-free, if
necessary)

2 tablespoons neutral-flavored oil
(coconut or canola oil works great)

Sprinkles (optional)

FOR THE FROSTING

1 scoop vanilla protein powder or
¼ cup softened cream cheese

1 to 2 tablespoons granulated
sweetener of choice

1 to 2 tablespoons cashew butter
(optional)

Milk, to thin out (dairy-free, if
necessary)

Preheat the oven to 350 degrees Fahrenheit. Grease a small 4-inch square or mini loaf pan with cooking spray and set it aside.

In a large mixing bowl, combine the dry ingredients and mix well.

In a separate bowl, add the egg, vanilla extract, and ¼ cup of milk and whisk lightly. Pour the milk mixture into the dry mixture, along with the oil. Mix well, until all the ingredients are fully incorporated. Stir in the sprinkles, if using, be-fore transferring the batter to the greased loaf pan. Bake for 12 to 15 minutes, or until a toothpick comes out clean from the center. Allow the blondies to cool completely.

While the blondies are cooling, make the frosting. In a small bowl, combine the protein powder with your granulated sweetener of choice and the nut butter, if using. Using a tablespoon at a time, slowly add your milk of choice until a frosting-like consistency remains. Top the cooled blondies with the frosting and refrigerate them for 30 minutes, until firm.

Cut the blondies into pieces and enjoy!

If you use the cream cheese frosting, you'll need less milk than if you use protein powder.

Depending on the protein powder you use, you may need a little more of your milk of choice for the batter.

FROSTED CINNAMON APPLE BARS ⓖⓢⓥⓟ

YIELD

4 bars

COOKING TIME

25 to 30 minutes, plus time to cool completely

NUTRITIONAL INFORMATION

Calories 318, Protein 18 grams, Fat 21 grams, Fiber 5 grams

INGREDIENTS

½ cup pitted dates

¾ cup almond butter

¼ cup unsweetened applesauce

¼ cup milk of choice (dairy-free, if necessary)

½ cup almond meal

2 tablespoons coconut flour

1½ teaspoons baking soda

1 teaspoon cinnamon

1½ teaspoons vanilla extract

¼ teaspoon sea salt

PROTEIN FROSTING

2 scoops vanilla protein powder

1 teaspoon cinnamon

2 tablespoons cashew butter, melted (optional)

1 tablespoon maple syrup (optional)

Milk of choice, as needed

Preheat the oven to 350 degrees Fahrenheit. Grease an 8 × 4-inch loaf pan.

Place the dates in a small bowl and fill the bowl with enough hot water to cover them. Let them sit for 10 minutes then drain the water.

In a food processor or blender, add the softened dates, almond butter, and applesauce. Process well, stopping to scrape down the sides. Slowly add milk and continue to process. Add the dry ingredients and process until they are completely mixed.

Pour the batter into the greased pan. Bake for 25 to 30 minutes, depending on your oven. Let the bars cool in the pan completely.

While the bars are cooling, make the frosting. In a small bowl, add your protein powder and cinnamon then mix well. Add the optional cashew butter and maple syrup, mixing until a crumbly texture remains. Slowly add your milk of choice until a batter is formed, then continue adding more until a thick, spreadable frosting remains.

You can omit the cashew butter and maple syrup from the frosting completely.

Bars should be kept in the refrigerator, and last up to 5 days. They are also freezer friendly, and I'd recommend you freeze them in individual portions. If you do choose to freeze them, omit the frosting.

Apple and cinnamon is like peanut butter and chocolate: a match made in edible heaven. I love these bars, as they are deceptively filling and can pass as a breakfast or a snack between meals. For those wanting an added boost of protein, the frosting is key here!

I was fortunate to spend a few months in Columbus, Ohio. It took me quite a while to put together the correlation between the city and this infamous sweet treat! Unlike a traditional buckeye, my version is packed with protein and has no added sugar. It also doesn't use any butter or condensed milk. It's perfect as a pre- or post-workout snack and the protein powder can be substituted for peanut flour for an even bigger peanut butter punch.

PEANUT BUTTER PROTEIN BUCKEYES ⑥⑤Ⓥ

YIELD

4 large buckeyes or 8 small buckeyes

COOKING TIME

15 to 20 minutes, plus time to firm up

NUTRITIONAL INFORMATION

Calories 118, Protein 5 grams,
Fat 8 grams, Fiber 1 gram

INGREDIENTS

¼ cup peanut butter

1 scoop protein powder
(32 to 34 grams; can substitute with
2 tablespoons of powdered peanut
butter/peanut flour)

Milk of choice, as needed

¼ cup chocolate chips of choice
(dairy-free/sugar-free, if necessary)

1 tablespoon coconut oil

*You will most likely not need to use
the full amount of the chocolate
coating. If desired, feel free to coat
each ball entirely in it.*

🅟 Swap out the peanut butter for
smooth almond butter or cashew
butter.

In a small mixing bowl, combine the peanut butter with the protein powder and mix very well. The mixture should be incredibly crumbly. Using a tablespoon at a time, add your milk of choice until a very thick batter remains. Form the batter into small balls and immediately place them in the freezer to firm up.

In a small microwave-safe bowl or on the stovetop, melt your chocolate chips together with the coconut oil. Allow the mixture to sit for 2 to 3 minutes to cool slightly. Remove the balls from the freezer and, using a spoon, dip half of each ball in the chocolate mixture until each buckeye has a half-moon choco-late coating. Refrigerate for 15 to 20 minutes more, until the chocolate has hardened.

PEANUT BUTTER PROTEIN CUPS ⓖⓥⓟ

YIELD

8 large cups, 16 small cups

COOKING TIME

30 minutes, plus additional time to firm up between steps

NUTRITIONAL INFORMATION

Calories 119, Protein 5 grams, Fat 7 grams, Fiber 1 gram

INGREDIENTS

½ cup drippy peanut butter (can substitute with another nut butter)

2 scoops vanilla protein powder (can substitute with ¼ cup peanut flour)

¼ cup milk of choice

⅔ cup chocolate chips of choice

1 teaspoon coconut oil

You can swap out the protein powder for peanut flour.

Feel free to add some sweetener to the filling (my protein powder was sweetened).

Ⓢ Use sugar-free baking chips.

Line an 8-count muffin tray with muffin liners and set it aside.

In a microwave-safe bowl or on the stovetop, melt the chocolate chips together with the coconut oil. Distribute three-quarters of the chocolate mixture evenly among the muffin tins, scraping the sides. Refrigerate for 10 to 20 minutes, until the chocolate hardens.

In a separate bowl, combine the peanut butter and protein powder until a crumbly mixture remains. Using a tablespoon at a time, add your milk of choice until a very thick batter is formed.

Remove the muffin tray from the fridge and ensure the chocolate has firmed up. Divide the peanut butter mixture evenly among the muffin tins. Reheat the remaining chocolate and cover each of the cups.

Refrigerate until the cups are firm.

The first time I went to America, I overloaded on peanut butter cups—I even brought back half a suitcase for all my friends back home to try! I kind of wish I hadn't, as they are super simple to make and this healthier version tastes just as good as its inspiration.

These snickerdoodle cake bars are the recipe to make when you want to convert someone to healthy eating. They don't taste the least bit healthy, and are a cross between an angel food cake and a muffin bar.

SNICKERDOODLE CAKE BARS ☺

YIELD

9 bars

COOKING TIME

30 to 35 minutes, plus time to cool completely

NUTRITIONAL INFORMATION

Calories 197, Protein 7 grams, Fat 2 grams, Fiber 3 grams

INGREDIENTS

1 cup gluten-free oat flour

Pinch sea salt

½ teaspoon baking soda

1 teaspoon cinnamon, plus more for dusting

1 to 2 tablespoons granulated sweetener of choice, plus more for dusting

2 large egg whites

¼ cup plain Greek yogurt (dairy-free, if necessary)

6 tablespoons maple syrup

½ teaspoon vanilla extract

1 cup unsweetened applesauce

¼ cup milk of choice (dairy-free, if necessary)

Melted coconut butter, to drizzle

These bars need to be kept refrigerated, and can be kept for up to 5 days. They are freezer friendly too: it's best to freeze them in individual portions for quick grab-and-go snacks or breakfasts.

Preheat the oven to 350 degrees Fahrenheit. Line a mini loaf pan with parchment paper or aluminum foil. Grease it lightly and set it aside.

In a large mixing bowl, add the dry ingredients and mix well. In a separate bowl, mix the wet ingredients until combined. Pour the wet mixture into the dry mixture and mix until fully incorporated.

Pour the batter into the lined baking dish or loaf pan and top with extra cinnamon. Bake for 30 to 35 minutes, or until a toothpick comes out clean. Allow the snickerdoodle to cool in the pan completely. Top with the optional coconut butter drizzle and cut into 9 bars. Dust bars with granulated sweetener.

FROZEN TREATS AND BEVERAGES

COOL MINT CHIP
ICE CREAM ⒢⒮ⓥ

YIELD

1 serving

COOKING TIME

5 minutes blending, plus time between blends to firm up

NUTRITIONAL INFORMATION

Calories 130, Protein 23 grams, Fat 0 gram, Fiber 1 gram

INGREDIENTS

1 cup plain yogurt (dairy-free, if necessary)

2 tablespoons granulated sweetener of choice or liquid sweetener equivalent

¼ teaspoon mint extract

¼ teaspoon vanilla extract

Chocolate chips

For a thicker ice cream, blend very slowly and for a short period of time. To enjoy this as a thick shake smoothie, blend until the ingredients are immersed.

Ⓟ This won't work with coconut milk (from neither a can nor a carton) but works with coconut yogurt. You will need to adjust the sweetener level, as I found the coconut taste overbearing. It also needs to thaw longer before scooping into bowls, otherwise it will be too icy.

I sometimes think that mint is like licorice: you either love it or hate it. Actually, I think licorice gets a little more flack, but that's a story for another day. Me? I am obsessed with all things mint. My all-time favorite candy bar is mint Aero (for my eighteenth birthday, my friends got me twenty family-sized blocks of it!). This simple mint-flavored ice cream is smooth, creamy, and is made in a blender. You can enjoy it ice cream style or as a thick smoothie, straight from the blender.

Mix all the ingredients, except for the chocolate chips, in a small bowl. Transfer the mixture to a freezer-friendly container or ice cube tray and place it in the freezer until frozen.

Remove the mixture from the freezer and place it in a high-speed blender and blend until your desired consistency is reached. Stir in the chocolate chips, scoop the ice cream into a bowl using an ice cream scoop, and enjoy!

FROZEN COFFEE 'CINO ⓖⓢⓥⓟ

YIELD

1 serving

COOKING TIME

5 minutes

NUTRITIONAL INFORMATION

Calories 151, Protein 25 grams,
Fat 4 grams, Fiber 2 grams

INGREDIENTS

1 scoop of vanilla protein powder
(32 to 34 grams)

1 cup milk of choice (dairy-free, if
necessary)

1 tablespoon instant coffee granules
(decaf works)

1 tablespoon granulated sweetener
of choice (optional)

Whipped topping, if desired

*For a thicker shake, swap out half of
the milk for ½ cup crushed ice.*

Coffee lovers, this one is for you!
I re-created my favorite coffee
shop drink, minus the usual sugar,
fat, and cream found in it. There is
no need for any fancy gadgets or
coffee-making tools—by letting it sit
once blended, it naturally creates a
delicious, creamy foam.

Add all the ingredients, except for the
whipped topping, into a high-speed blender.
Blend for under a minute, until the ingredients are fully immersed. Transfer the
mixture to a tall glass and let it sit for 1 to 2
minutes, for the foam to separate. Top with
whipped topping and enjoy!

STRAWBERRIES AND CREAM FROZEN YOGURT ⓖⓢ

YIELD

1 serving

COOKING TIME

5 minutes, plus 2 hours to freeze and thaw

NUTRITIONAL INFORMATION

Calories 250, Protein 31 grams, Fat 4 grams, Fiber 4 grams

INGREDIENTS

1 cup low-fat cottage cheese

1 cup frozen strawberries

⅔ cup milk of choice

½ teaspoon vanilla extract

2 tablespoons liquid zero-calorie sweetener

Ⓥ Substitute the cottage cheese for a cultured soy yogurt or dairy-free yogurt. However, it won't thicken as well as with cottage cheese.

Ⓟ Swap the cottage cheese for coconut yogurt and ensure it is sweet enough before freezing. I tried it with coconut milk (canned) but it was too rich and difficult to thaw.

I don't even want to think about how much money I spent at those silly self-serve frozen yogurt places. Whenever a craving hit, I'd load up one of those small cups and, well . . . ten dollars later. With just a blender, I can have a smooth, creamy, and thick frozen yogurt. Not only that, but without all the excess sugar!

Add all the ingredients to a blender and process until the mixture is thick and smooth.

Remove the mixture from the blender and place it in a freezer-friendly tray for 2 hours, or until it's set. Once it's set, remove it from the freezer and allow it to defrost slightly. Use a wet ice cream scoop and serve in a bowl.

THICK AND CREAMY
MOCHA ICE CREAM Ⓖ Ⓢ Ⓥ Ⓟ

YIELD

1 serving

COOKING TIME

5 minutes

NUTRITIONAL INFORMATION

Calories 248, Protein 26 grams,
Fat 2 grams, Fiber 5 grams

INGREDIENTS

1½ cups precooked frozen sweet
potato chunks

1 scoop chocolate protein powder
(32 to 34 grams)

2 tablespoons granulated or liquid
sweetener of choice (I prefer honey)

¼ cup milk of choice (dairy-free, if
necessary)

1 teaspoon coffee extract (can
substitute with instant coffee)

*For a thicker, more ice cream–like
texture, freeze the mocha for an
hour prior to consuming.*

*For a smoothie-like texture, increase
the milk of your choice by ¼ cup.*

*Not a fan of sweet potato? Feel free
to substitute with pumpkin, berries,
or bananas!*

Sometimes the strangest of ingredients lead to the best things. I never would have thought that a sweet potato could be used in a frozen dessert, let alone that I would not be able to even tell! I added some coffee extract to give it a mocha flavor (paired with the chocolate protein powder), but feel free to omit to keep it completely chocolate.

In a high-speed blender or food processor, add all the ingredients and blend until the mixture is thick and creamy.

Transfer to a bowl and enjoy!

VANILLA CAKE BATTER
MILK SHAKE Ⓖ Ⓢ Ⓥ Ⓟ

YIELD

1 serving

COOKING TIME

5 minutes, or longer for thicker shake

NUTRITIONAL INFORMATION

Calories 364, Protein 33 grams,
Fat 20 grams, Fiber 7 grams

INGREDIENTS

⅔ cup milk of choice (dairy-free,
if necessary)

⅓ cup ice cubes

2 tablespoons nut butter of choice

1 tablespoon pure maple syrup or
granulated sweetener of choice

1 teaspoon vanilla extract

1 scoop vanilla protein powder
(32 to 34 grams, optional)

1 tablespoon coconut flour or gluten-
free rolled oats

*Protein powder can be substituted
with 1 scoop of collagen.*

*For a thicker shake, refrigerate for
30 minutes prior to drinking (ensure
coconut flour or oats are used).*

Vanilla milk shakes are my
favorite, because they are so
versatile. You can enjoy them
on their own and, if you want a
different flavor profile, it's easy to do.
Chocolate cake batter? Add a dash
of cocoa powder. Cinnamon spiked?
You bet! You can even make it fruit
flavored too.

Add all the ingredients to a high-speed
blender and blend until fully immersed.
Serve immediately!

Acknowledgments

No job—or cookbook—can be completed successfully without a solid support network.

I'd like to thank my literary agent, MacKenzie Fraser-Bub. I am so thankful you saw something in me, as well as my recipes, and brought it to a wider audience. And also for your immense help with EVERYTHING—right down to television recommendations (mindless or not).

I'd like to thank my immediate family—my mum, sister, dad, and, of course, my grandma, who's had nothing but praise for my recipes (mostly because she is too kind to ever say anything negative).

I'd like to thank all my friends for their support, especially those who have played guinea pig to all the creations you'll find in this book. In no particular order, thank you Ingrid Cowley, Lauren Hildebrand, Sophie Danner, Alexis Lauren Joseph, Julia Dorfschmidt, Natalie Thomas, Bec Kerr, and Andria Kalliakoudis.

Most of all, I'd like to thank all my readers. It humbles me that several million of you come to my website each month, and continue to do so regularly. More importantly, nothing makes me happier than the daily emails, messages, and pictures of YOUR re-creations of my recipes. Without you, I wouldn't have had the courage, motivation, or drive to continue experimenting and developing recipes.

I hope you enjoy this cookbook and, as always, never hesitate to contact me if you are having trouble with any of the recipes or to suggest potential alternatives.

Index